Python for Finance

Jay Chen, PhD, CFA

ii

To Ping, Andrew, and Abigail,
my forever love

Contents

1 **Python Installation**   1
    1.1   Exercise   2

2 **Python Basics: Numbers and Expressions**   5
    2.1   Numbers   5
    2.2   Operators   6
    2.3   Assignment   7
    2.4   Getting Input from the User   8
    2.5   .py   9
    2.6   Exercises   10

3 **Python Basics: Strings and Lists**   13
    3.1   Strings   13
    3.2   Immutable Sequences and Indexing   14
    3.3   Methods   15
    3.4   Lists   16
    3.5   What about Tuples and Dictionaries?   18
    3.6   Exercises   18

4 **Control Flow: If Statements**   21
    4.1   Branching with If   21
    4.2   elif   22
    4.3   Boolean Tests and Multiple Conditions   22
    4.4   Exercises   24

5 **Control Flow: While Loops**   27
    5.1   While Loops   27
    5.2   Exit a While Loop   28
    5.3   Getting Stuck in a Loop   29
    5.4   Unknown Rounds of Repetition   29
    5.5   Exercises   30

6 Control Flow: For Loops   **33**
   6.1 For Loops 33
   6.2 range( ) 34
   6.3 The Iterator 35
   6.4 Exercises 35

7 Financial Application: Monte Carlo Simulations   **39**
   7.1 Throwing a Dice 39
   7.2 Wealth Accumulation 40
   7.3 Exercises 41

8 User-Defined Functions   **45**
   8.1 Functions as a Block 45
   8.2 User-Defined Functions as Modules 46
   8.3 Exercises 46

9 Plotting   **51**
   9.1 X-Y Scatter Plot 51
   9.2 Color and Line Type 52
   9.3 Histogram 53
   9.4 Labeling and Other Settings 53
   9.5 Exercises 54

10 Numerical Methods   **57**
   10.1 Cubic Roots 57
   10.2 Quadratic Equations 58
   10.3 Exercises 60

11 Pandas: Data Structure   **65**
   11.1 DataFrame 65
   11.2 Data Cleanup 67
   11.3 DataFrame Index 68
   11.4 Plotting 69
   11.5 DataFrame from Scratch 70
   11.6 Export a csv File 71
   11.7 Exercises 71

12 Pandas: Financial Data   **73**
   12.1 Historical Stock Prices from Yahoo! Finance® 73
   12.2 Stock Prices as a DataFrame Object 74
   12.3 More Indexing 75
   12.4 Summary Statistics 76

12.5 Time Series 77
12.6 Exercises 78

13 Financial Application: Technical Analysis   **81**
13.1 Filter Rules 81
13.2 Simple Moving Average 84
13.3 Exercises 85

14 Pandas: Data and Dictionaries   **87**
14.1 Dynamic Code Generation with exec( ) 87
14.2 Merging Data 88
14.3 Bar Charts as a Tool to Visualize Data 89
14.4 Dictionaries 90
14.5 Exercises 93

15 Pandas: Groupby   **95**
15.1 A Groupby Example of the S&P 500 95
15.2 Groupby and Resample 98
15.3 Exercises 99

16 Ordinary Least Squares Regression   **101**
16.1 OLS with statsmodels 101
16.2 CAPM Regression 104
16.3 Fama and French Three-Factor Model 106
16.4 Logistic Regression 107
16.5 Exercises 108

17 Time Series Fitting   **111**
17.1 An AR Model with statsmodels.tsa 111
17.2 Autocorrelation Functions 112
17.3 Augmented Dickey-Fuller Test for Unit Root 114
17.4 ARIMA 116
17.5 Model Selection 116
17.6 Forecast and Forecast Errors 120
17.7 Exercises 122

18 Optimization   **125**
18.1 A Four-Asset Portfolio 125
18.2 Brute Force Grid Search 127
18.3 Optimization with Scipy 129
18.4 Exercises 131

19 Final Words   **135**

Introduction

This book is for financial practitioners and young economists who don't have experience with coding but want to learn how to code for their job. It is also ideal for graduate students or senior undergrads to learn how to code before starting his/her graduate study. As an introductory text, this book is by no means comprehensive. But I can assure you that if you study the chapters and carefully go through the exercises, you will be ready to use Python at work.

There are two principles I see in learning to code: (1) The best way to learn coding is to work on exercises and (2) the biggest obstacle is often the jargon. Having these principles in mind, I designed the book to be light on explanations of terms and heavy on exercises. In the age of Google and Stack Overflow, it is unwise to force feed a beginner with intimidating terms. Unless a term is absolutely in need of an explanation, I focus only on its use, not the definition. Whenever I introduce a new concept or method, I always accompany it with a few exercises in the end of the chapter.

Sample solutions to some of the questions are posted on this book's website (csandaa.com /python-book). The remaining sample solutions are only provided to instructors who adopt this book as a textbook.

Cohan Lin designed the cover and Matthew Appler edited the text. I am grateful for their work. Any error, however, is mine. If you have any suggestions or find any error in my book, please send me your comment by email (amazingcoestartup@gmail.com).

I hope you will soon find the joy of coding in Python!

Jay Chen, PhD, CFA
Elnora H. and William B. Quarton Associate Professor of Finance
Coe College, Cedar Rapids, Iowa

October 10, 2019

Chapter 1

Python Installation

We will use Python 3.6. There are quite a few differences between Python 2.X and Python 3.X. But the practitioners are gradually shifting to the newer 3.X. In some cases, the older 2.X still has more libraries and functions to use, but the shift to the newer version should be complete soon.

Python benefits greatly from the open-source software movement. Many programmers continue to contribute to the development of Python. As more people use it, it becomes even more powerful. With more applications in different areas, the virtuous cycle continues. I rely on many of the free resources developed by previous developers. Now even the coding environment is free and no less powerful than for-fee ones. I am indebted to these Python pioneers and enthusiasts.

This book solely uses **Anaconda's spyder** as our coding environment. I also highly recommend **repl.it** (https://repl.it), an online coding environment, for its ability of real-time collaboration with other coders and its increasing number of libraries.

Please go to www.anaconda.com to download the integrated development environment (IDE), **Anaconda**. The installation is painless and self-explanatory, regardless of your hardware specification. Once you launch the **Anaconda Navigator**, you will see a collection of applications. We will use **spyder** as the primary IDE.

A typical spyder window is shown in the next page. In spyder, we shall keep only two panes opened to make the interface clean: ① the editor and ② IPython Console. You can close all other panes by unchecking them in **view** > **panes** in the menu bar of spyder.

The editor is where you create and edit your code. Spyder's editor offers more than standard word processing functions. It also gives you warnings and in-line help when you code. IPython stands for interactive Python. Here you feed lines of code in and receive feedback right away. You can execute line commands one at a time, too. Try using it as a calculator.

For example, type in IPython Console

In   [1]: 1 + 1

You will get

Out [1]: 2

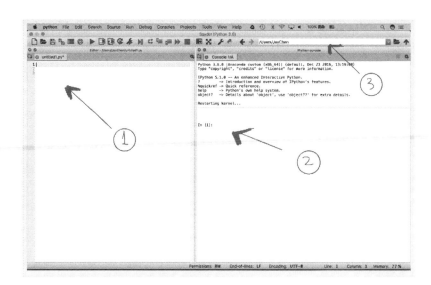

③ in the graph points to the working directory. When you work on data files, you want to make sure the data files are in the same working directory as your code.

The rest of the interface is similar to what you see in many of the off-the-shelf software. For special commands that are not self-explanatory, I will explain them when they are used.

1.1   Exercise

1. Generating *Hello World* on the screen is often considered the first code in learning a programming language. Let's try it in IPython Console and also the editor.

   (a) Type in IPython Console:

In [1]: print("Hello World")

(b) Type the same thing in the editor and run the file. You can save the file and run the whole thing or highlight and select specific lines you need and run them. Just go to **Run** in the menu bar.

When you save a file, make sure it has .py extension.

Try! The beauty of an IDE like spyder is to allow the user to have trials and errors freely.

Chapter 2

Python Basics: Numbers and Expressions

Before we speak the Python language, let's first know some basic vocabulary and grammar.

2.1   Numbers

Computers use the language of math. Each line of command that the user feeds the computer takes the form of a mathematical expression. An expression typically has two parts: **objects** and **operators**. For instance, in the expression **3 + 5**, **3** and **5** are objects and **+** is an operator.

There are various types of objects in Python. I will start with the object **numbers**. Numbers can be an integer type (numbers without decimal points) or a floating number type (numbers with decimal points). Python recognizes the type the first time a number is used or assigned. Try in IPython Console the following commands.

In   [1]: 3.5*5
Out [1]: 17.5

In   [2]: 3*5
Out [2]: 15

Also try this function **type( )**. Functions as black boxes. You give input to the black boxes and receive output from them. We will learn more about functions in later chapters. At this moment, all you need to know is that a function has a name and it takes input (also known as arguments or parameters) from inside the parenthesis. See the following two examples.

```
In   [3]: type(3*5)
Out [3]: int
```

```
In   [4]: type(3.5*5)
Out [4]: float
```

2.2   Operators

Typical math operators such as $+, -, \times, \div$ are used directly, but $\times$ is represented by $*$ and $\div$ by $/$. You follow the same order of operations (PEDMAS: parentheses, exponents, multiplication and division, and addition and subtraction) as you do in math.

Sometimes we need to compare numbers. Try these command lines:

```
In   [5]: 3 > 4
In   [6]: 3 >= 4
In   [7]: 3 < 4
In   [8]: 3 <= 4
In   [9]: 3 != 4
In   [10]: 3 == 4
```

In output 5-10, they are either **True** or **False**. True and False constitute a special object called **bool**, standing for Boolean. They will be very useful when it comes to logical tests, which I will discuss soon.

The last two comparison operators need some explanation. != means **not equal to**. In programming languages, a single equal sign is not equating two things. It means assigning things on the right to things on the left (more on that in the next section.) Two equal signs do the work for equating.

Addition, subtraction, and multiplication are straightforward, but division is tricky. There are three types of division:

```
In   [11]: 3 / 4
Out [11]: 0.75
```

```
In   [12]: 3//4
Out [12]: 0
```

In [13]: **3 % 4**
Out [13]: **3**

As you see in the output, / is the normal division, // does division but returns the quotient, and %, also known as the modulus operator, returns the remainder.

In fact, multiplication has some variations, too. Try

In [14]: **3**4**
Out [14]: **81**

[handwritten: 3^4]   *[handwritten: print (3**4)]*

In [15]: **3**0.5**
Out [15]: **1.7320508075688772**

[handwritten: $\sqrt{3}$]

Line 14 means 3^4 and 15 means $\sqrt{3}$. So ****** performs the exponential (power) calculation in Python.

2.3   Assignment

When we do math, we don't just operate on numbers. We also work on variables. In Python, creating a variable is straightforward. You assign a value to a variable name like this:

In [16]: **a = 5**

You should read the line as "Variable **a** gets value 5." By doing so, you create a variable called **a** and at the same time give it a numeric value of 5. **Assignment** or the single equal sign = is not performing an algebraic equality. Remind yourself that when you want an equality in Python, you use double equal signs ==. This concept is lethally important in coding. It is therefore worthy of repeating. Check Exercises 2 and 3 of this Chapter now.

When you assign a value to a variable, IPython Console does not show anything, but you can call or print[1] the variable.

In [17]: **a**
Out [17]: **5**

---

[1]**print( )**, as we saw in Chapter 1, is a function that prints out the value of the argument(s) inside the parenthsis.

In   [18]: print(a)
5

Python will store the value of your variable until you re-assign a new value to it. Try these:

In   [19]: b = 6
In   [20]: c = a + b
In   [21]: c
Out [21]: 11

If you assign a new value to **a**, what happens to **c**?

In   [22]: a = 7
In   [23]: c
Out [23]: 11

This is the **pointer** concept in coding. The values and variables are associated with assignment statements. Line 20 doesn't tell Python to always perform the addition of **a** and **b** when evaluating the value of **c**. It assigns value of 11 to **c** and **c** carries 11 until further notice.

If you want **c** to reflect the change of value in **a**, you need to assign the result of the addition again.

In   [24]: c = a + b
In   [25]: c
Out [25]: 13

2.4   Getting Input from the User

To have a dynamic interaction between a computer program and the user, we can use the **input( )** function. For example,

In   [26]: x = input("Give me a number: ")

The argument (the thing you enter in the parenthesis of the function) for **input( )** is the text prompt, a message intended for the user. It must be enclosed in quotation marks. Python treats ' ' (apostrophes) and " " (quotation marks) identically. But for the same quote, you need to be consistent. You can't mix them in the same quote.

Once the user types in something, that something is assigned to your variable **x**. That something might look like a number, but **input( )** automatically treats the user input as a string (text) object. I will cover string objects in the next chapter. For now, we need to convert the user input into a number before using it.

Give me a number: 5
In   [27]: print(x)
5
In   [28]: type(x)
Out [28]: str

We need to **cast** the variable by using **float( )** or **int( )**. Casting is to covert an object from one type to another.

In   [29]: x = float(x)
In   [30]: print(x)
5.0
In   [31]: type(x)
Out [31]: float

In line 29, the concept of assignment again must be clearly understood. This is how you understand the line: you cast the string variable **x** to a float object by using **float( )** and then assign it back to variable **x**.

2.5   .py

Instead of writing one line at a time in IPython Console, you can type up a few lines in the editor. Then save it as a .py file. Then run the batch of lines together. Try typing the following into the editor:

01 #This line does not count.
02 print("a+b")
03 a = float(input("a?: "))
04 b = float(input("b?: "))
05 print("a+b=")
06 print(a+b)

Let me explain these lines a bit. The script starts in line 1, which literally asks the computer to skip this line. Any line of code starts with the hashtag # (or called the pound sign) will be ignored by Python. You use this to write notes for yourself or collaborators. If you have a lot to say that should not be counted as code, you can use two sets of three consecutive apostrophes or quotation marks to enclose the comments.

Line 3 employs two functions and one assignment at the same time. You start from the right-hand side and from the most inner part of the parentheses. **input( )** asks for the user input and **float( )** converts that input into a floating number immediately. The floating number then is assigned to the variable **a**.

To run multiple lines from the editor, you either select the lines to be executed and **Run selection or current line** from **Run** in the menu bar or save the script as a file and then run the file from **Run** in the menu bar. The green triangle button also indicates **Run**.

When you save a Python script, make sure you have .py extension. Files with .py extension can be recognized by any Python programs, although they are most of the time simple text files.

2.6   Exercises

Questions with asterisks have sample solutions on the book's website (www.csandaa.com/python-book).

1.* Use IPython Console as a calculator and find answers for the following expressions.

  (a) $\dfrac{1 + 3 \times 5}{4 \times 6 + 2}$. print(1+3*5/4*6+2)

  (b) $\sqrt{3 + 6(4 \div 2)}$. print((3+6)*4/2**0.5)

  (c) $\sqrt{7 + 9} \times 2$. print((7+9)**0.5*2)

2. Do the following two lines in IPython Console. What does the second line mean and what is the value of **x** now?

  In   [1]: x = 5   assignment
  In   [2]: x = x + 5   10

  Many people have a hard time getting the assignment concept and give up on coding. If you can't understand these two lines, you need to re-learn the meaning of = and ==.

3.* Swapping values. After writing the following lines in IPython Console, you realize you have mistakenly swapped the values.

  In   [1]: x = 3
  In   [2]: y = 5

You understand the concept of assignment, so you go ahead and write two more lines to swap the values back.

In   [3]: x = y
In   [4]: y = x

But you do not get the results you want. What is going on? How do you correctly swap the values of **x** and **y**?

4. Write a .py file to complete the following task: Ask the user to provide a number. You print out the square root of such a number.

5.* Write a .py file to complete the following task: Ask the user for the temperature in Celsius and print out the temperature in Fahrenheit. The formula is $F = 32 + C \times \frac{9}{5}$, where F is the temperature in Fahrenheit and C Celsius.

6. Write a .py file to report the roots of any quadratic equation with coefficients provided by the user. The formula for a quadratic equation roots: For $ax^2 + bx + c = 0$,
$$x = \frac{-b \pm \sqrt{b^2 - 4ac}}{2a}.$$

Chapter 3

Python Basics: Strings and Lists

3.1 Strings

Text strings, or simply **strings**, are distinctively different from the number object. They start out as messages for and by the users, but are much more than that. When strings are shown or used in code, they are enclosed in two apostrophes or quotation marks. Python treats the two ways of quoting identically, but you need to be consistent when applying them to a string object.

We can assign a string as a value to a variable. For example,

```
In   [1]: a = "15"
In   [2]: a
Out [2]: '15'
```

It doesn't matter whether it looks like a number or text. As long as it is in quotes, it is a string. You can cast strings to numbers and cast them back by using **float( )**, **int( )** and **str( )**. Try these in IPython Console.

```
In   [3]: a = float(a)
In   [4]: type(a)
Out [4]: float
```

```
In   [5]: a = str(a)
In   [6]: type(a)
Out [6]: str
```

You can also concatenate strings (adding two or more strings) by "adding" them together.

For example,

In   [7]: x = "P"+"y"+"t"+"h"+"o"+"n"
In   [8]: print(x)
Python

3.2   Immutable Sequences and Indexing

One feature that strings have but numbers don't is that they are **sequences**. As you see in
the concatenation example, we can treat a string as a sequence of characters. For sequences
in Python, you can actually count the elements in them with an order. Sequences also have
a **length**. To figure out how long a sequence is, we can use the function **len( )**.

In   [9]: len(x)   *print (len (x)))*
Out [9]: 6

Since sequences have orders, they can be indexed. In Python, a square bracket immediately
following a sequence object is used for indexing.

In   [10]: x[2]   *print x[2]*
Out [10]: 't'   *0,1,2,etc.*

Note that [2] indicates the third place in the string. It calls the third characther in the string
"Python". This is because **computer scientists always count from 0.** The previous
sentence is in bold letters because that is something coding novices are not familiar with
and worth emphasizing.

We can also slice the sequence by

In   [11]: y = x[0: 2]
In   [12]: y
Out [12]: 'Py'

The slicing command [start, end] does **not** include **end**. There are a few fancier ways to
slice and dice a sequence. Let's try all of them.

Select the whole sequence:

In   [13]: z = x[0:]
In   [14]: z

Out [14]: 'Python'

Select the whole sequence except the last element:

In   [15]: z = x[0: -1]   *Subtracts position starting from end*
In   [16]: z
Out [16]: 'Pytho'

Note that -1 means the last item in the sequence. Line 15 is the same as this:

In   [17]: z = x[: -1]
In   [18]: z
Out [18]: 'Pytho'

Although it is convenient to call, reference or use an individual character in a string, you **cannot** change the content of a string by assigning a new value to a specific location in a string. For example,

In   [19]: x[2] ="a"

You will get an error message:

TypeError: 'str' object does not support item assignment

This is because strings are **immutable**. Immutability is to protect the string objects from potential security problems.

3.3   Methods

However, if you want to change the content of immutable objects, you need applicable functions. For strings, you can do character replacement with the method **.replace("to be replaced", "replace with")**. A method is an object-specific function. You use a method the same way as a function: you call it by its name and supply arguments (or parameters) in the ensuing parenthesis. But you also attach the function directly to the object by **object.method( )**. Here is the .replace( ) example.

In   [20]: x.replace("o", "q")   *print (x.replace("o", "q"))*
Out [20]: 'Pythqn'
In   [21]: x   *but goes back to normal w/o .replace"*
Out [21]: 'Python'

Note that Line 20 creates a new value but it is not assigned to anything. Since strings are immutable, **x** still carries the old value. If you want to replace the old value, you need to do

```
In   [22]: x = x.replace("o", "q")
In   [23]: x
Out [23]: 'Pythqn'
```

Another useful method helps you find the first location of a specific character or text in a string: **.find("string to be found")**.

```
In   [24]: x.find("P")          Case sensitive or will [out -1"
Out [24]: 0
In   [25]: x.find("Py")
Out [25]: 0
```

In Exercise 6 of this chapter, I will discuss a few more useful string methods.

3.4   Lists

Lists are **mutable** sequences. They have powerful uses in Python because of their flexibility. To generate a list, we use square brackets and separate the items in the list with commas. When lists show up, they are always enclosed in square brackets.

```
In   [26]: xx = [3, 4, 5]
In   [27]: xx
Out [27]: [3, 4, 5]

In   [28]: yy = ["a", "b", "c"]
In   [29]: yy
Out [29]: ['a', 'b', 'c']
```

You can mix types in a list.

```
In   [30]: zz = [3, "a", 5]
In   [31]: zz
Out [31]: [3, 'a', 5]
```

Lists are so flexible that you can even have a list in a list.

In   [32]: xxx = [[3, 4, 5], "b", "c"]
In   [33]: xxx
Out [33]: [[3, 4, 5], 'b', 'c']

Since lists are also sequences, indexing and slicing methods we use on strings are also applicable on lists. The **len( )** function also works on lists.

In   [34]: xxx = xxx[0: 2]
In   [34]: xxx
Out [34]: [[3, 4, 5], 'b']

In   [35]: xxx[0]
Out [35]: [3, 4, 5]
In   [36]: xxx[0][0]
Out [36]: 3

In   [37]: len(xxx)
Out [37]: 2

Later on we will create many lists to store values of certain operations. We often start with an empty list a list and add values as we go. An important philosophy of Python is being intuitive. So when we want to start an empty list, we want to try square brackets with nothing in it. That is exactly how you create an empty list.

In   [38]: A = [ ]
In   [39]: A
Out [39]: [ ]

In   [40]: empty = [ ]

Lists themselves have useful methods.

In   [41]: empty.append(100)
In   [42]: empty
Out [42]: [100]

Note that you cannot directly assign **list.append()** to a new variable.

In   [43]: empty.remove(100)
In   [44]: empty
Out [44]: [ ]

This method remove the value 100 from your list. If your list have multiple values of 100, it removes the first one only.

If you want to delete an item from a list by its location, you can use the **del** command.

```
In   [45]: empty.append(100)
In   [46]: del empty[0]
In   [47]: empty
Out  [47]: [ ]
```

We end this chapter with a nice connection between strings and lists.

```
In   [48]: xyz = list("Python")
In   [49]: xyz
Out  [48]: ['P', 'y', 't', 'h', 'o', 'n']
```

3.5   What about Tuples and Dictionaries?

I have covered most of the basic objects we will use in this book. But if you had some knowledge about Python before using this book, you know I left out two other critical objects—**tuples** and **dictionaries**.

Tuples are objects similar to lists. They are enclosed with parentheses, instead of square brackets. More importantly, they are **immutable**, meaning the elements in them can't be altered. Given the limitations of tuples and their largely overlapped uses with lists, I won't use tuples in this book.

Dictionaries, however, are powerful and will be used in this book. I will discuss the use of them in Chapter 14.

3.6   Exercises

Questions with asterisks have sample solutions on the book's website (www.csandaa.com/python-book).

1.* Write a Python program to ask the user for a word. Report back to the user by printing the number of letters in the word.

2. Write a Python program to replace all "s" with "$" in a string supplied by the user.

3. Write a Python program to delete all "a" in a string supplied by the user.

4.* Write a Python program to complete the following task.

    (a) Ask the user for a word three separate times.

    (b) Put those words in a list.

    (c) Print the list.

    (d) Remove the first word in the list.

    (e) Print the shortened list.

5. The Caesar Cipher. Julius Caesar was said to encode the messages he sent to the generals on the battlefield by replacing the alphabets with those a few places back in the order. For example, letter **a** is replaced with **c** if he and the generals agreed on two place shift. The generals decoded the messages by shifting the alphabets back. Let's write a program to create a simple version of the Caesar Cipher.

    (a) Ask the user for a three letter word.

    (b) Convert each letter to an ASCII code by using **ord()**. Now each letter carries a number.

    (c) Add 5 to each number.

    (d) Use **chr()** to convert the numbers to characters, one at a time.

    (e) Concatenate the new three characters and print out the message.

    (f) How do you decode the message? Write another program for decoding.

6.* String and list methods. Objects often have object-specific operations you can work on. You can treat these as built-in functions. The way to call these functions, known as methods, is to use **object.function**, as you see in the main text. Here you can practice some other useful methods of the string and list objects.

    (a) string.lower( ): return string letters into lower cases.

    (b) string.upper( ): return string letters into upper cases.

    (c) list.max( ): return the largest value.

    (d) list.min( ): return the smallest value.

    (e) list.sort( ): return the list in ascending order.

    (f) list.sort(reverse = True): return the list in descending order.

Chapter 4

Control Flow: If Statements

4.1   Branching with If

Python processes lines of code in the order that they appear. But coders frequently have to control the flow, either to branch out or to temporarily interrupt the flow. You can picture the order of processing as a decision tree. If you have to move down different branches given different conditions, you use **if statements**.

If statements are everywhere around you. When you unlock your smartphone with your finger, the phone is doing an if statement: "If" the fingerprint matches the owner's, unlock; otherwise (else), remain locked. These types of logical tests are critical in coding and a natural extension of how our brains work. For example, when you walk on the street, you turn your head, "if" you hear your name being called. In other words, your ears and brain are constantly doing an if statement.

Doing an if statement also means having a logical test. When a condition is met, our logical test of the condition returns **True**). And if it is not met, the test returns (**False**). As you might recall True/False themselves form an object called **bool** and the logical test is called a **boolean** test.

In a nutshell, an if statement tests a condition, and then the computer decides the next step based on the True/False test result.

Let's understand how Python does this logical test. Try this block of code.

```
01 age = int(input("Tell me your age: "))
02 if age > 25:
03     print("You are full of wisdom.")
04 else:
```

21

```
05       print("You are full of energy.")
```

A few things to note about this block of code. **if** starts the first line of a block. We always use the punctuation mark colon **:** at the end of the first line of a block to tell Python that the following is part of a block.

Codes inside a block must be indented by 4 spaces (or 1 tab). For nested blocks, you indent the lines by another 4 spaces.

else is optional. If you don't want Python to do anything in the alternative branch, you can leave out else.

4.2   elif

Python tests the condition in the if line (**age > 25** in this case). If the condition is true, it runs the if block. Otherwise, it moves to the else block. If you have more than two branches, the second option uses **elif**. You can have an unlimited amount of **elif** and leave the last option to else. For example,

```
06 age = int(input("Tell me your age: "))
07 if age < 25:
08       print("You are young.")
09 elif age > 60:
10       print("You are full of wisdom.")
09 else:
10       print("You are busy in life.")
```

There is no limit as to how many elif you can have in your code.

4.3   Boolean Tests and Multiple Conditions

The logical test for an if statement can be a complicated one. For example, a bank might approve a loan if the borrower has a credit score greater than 800 **and** a steady job. The bank's loan officer is then doing an if statement with multiple conditions. Python uses the English word **and** for combining two conditions. Very intuitive! A code might be like the following.

```
11 if credit_score > 800 and job =="Yes" :
12      print("Loan is approved.")
13 else:
14       print("Not approved")
```

The if statement will only proceed to line 12 if both conditions are met.

If, however, another bank that is more relaxed in its lending practice, it might ask if the person has either a credit score greater than 800 **or** a steady job. The previous example asks for the intersection of the two events' outcome, but this one the union. Therefore, it encompasses more possibilities.

```
15 if credit_score > 800 or job =="Yes" :
16      print("Loan is approved.")
17 else:
18       print("Not approved")
```

Such multiple condition tests are known as boolean tests. They can get complicated and some programmers encourage novices to memorize the outcome of these and's and or's. But I believe they should be used just like how you say them. If the tests are going beyond the intuition, stop. Break down your decision trees into more branches. Simplicity not only works in writing, but also coding.

Let's look at another example that involves an intuitive boolean test. A history teacher gives a quiz to students, but sometimes the answer is not what is expected.

```
19 print("Which of the following was not a U.S. President?")
20 print("a. Alexander Hamilton")
21 print("b. George Washington")
22 print("c. John Adams")
23 print("d. Thomas Jefferson")
24
25 answer = input("Your answer is: ")
26
27 if answer not in "abcd":
28      print("Please only enter a, b, c, or d.")
29 elif answer == "a":
30      print("Great. You are right.")
31 else:
32      print("I am sorry. You are wrong.")
```

Line 27's **not in** test will return True, if the answer is outside the selection. Here I also utilize the string object's sequence feature. Python will check the characters in the string one at a time.

If statements are compatible with human's logical thinking, but it takes practice to get the syntax of them right. Do the exercises to improve your skill.

4.4   Exercises

Questions with asterisks have sample solutions on the book's website (www.csandaa.com/python-book).

1. Write a Python program to determine whether a number is even. The number is supplied by the user through **input( )**. Hint: the modulus operator **%** that does division but returns the remainder is useful here.

2.* Write a Python program to determine whether a year is a leap year or not.

3. If today is Monday, write a Python program to determine what day it is **n** days from now. **n** is supplied by the user.

4. Write a Python program to determine whether a number is both divisible by 2 and 3. The number is supplied by the user through **input( )**.

5. Look at the following code.

   ```
   1 if True:
   2      print("Python is fun.")
   3 else:
   4      print("Python is boring.")
   ```

   What do you think the execution outcome will be? Why?

6. A dog's age. For the first two years, a dog year is equal to 10.5 human years. After that, each dog year equals 4 human years. For example, if a dog lives for 15 years, it is 73 years old by human standard. Write a Python program to determine how old a dog is, given the years it has lived in this world.

7. Sorting (i). Write a Python program to sort three numbers (a, b, and c) supplied by the user. Report the largest number back. In this program, your algorithm is to compare them one at a time.

8.* Sorting (ii). Write a Python program to sort three numbers (a, b, and c) supplied by the user. Report the largest number back. In this program, your algorithm is to work out a decision tree by comparing a and b first.

9. Sorting (iii). Write a Python program to sort three numbers (a, b, and c) supplied by the user. Report the largest number back. In this program, your algorithm is to create a temporary placeholder called **big**. Whichever number is bigger than **big** becomes the new **big**.

10. Rock-paper-scissors. Write a Python program to play a rock-paper-scissors game. The user provides both players' choices and your program returns the result.

11. Rock-paper-scissors revisit. Now your program will play with the user. Your program should randomly choose from a list ["**rock**", "**paper**", "**scissors**"] after the user picks the handsign. Your program should then tell whether the user or the computer wins. You will need to import[1] the **numpy** library to use the random choice function.

import numpy as np
computer_pick = np.random.choice(["rock", "paper", "scissors"])

12.* Pig Latin. Write a Python program to convert an ordinary English word, supplied by the user, to Pig Latin. The Pig Latin's rule is to move the first letter to the end and add "ay" after it, if the first letter is a consonant. If it is a vowel, just add "hay" to the end of the word.

13. Zeller's algorithm. In the late 19th century, Christian Zeller uncovered a method to determine the day of the week for any day in time. His method calculates a number **h**. If **h** is 0, it is a Saturday. If the number is 1, it is a Sunday, etc. Here are the steps you need to calculate **h**. Write a Python program to implement this algorithm.

   (a) $h = [q + int(\frac{13(m+1)}{5}) + k + int(\frac{k}{4}) + int(\frac{j}{4}) - 2j]\%7$

   (b) q = day of the month and m is the month. 3 is March, 4 April, etc. But note that January is 13, February 14 of the previous year.

   (c) k is the year of the century. So for 12/12/2015, $q = 12, m = 12, k = 15$ and For 2/12/2015, $q = 12, m = 14, k = 14$.

   (d) j is the zero-based century. For example, j for 2015 is 20.

---

[1]This is the first time we **import** functions from a library. Python 3.6 has many built-in ones, such as print( ) and len( ). There are literally millions of Python functions. It is not efficient or compatible to include all of them. Importing on demand is thus preferable. To distinguish between functions that are built-in and those that are imported, we add a prefix to the functions that are imported and used for the ease of understanding code. So in this example, we give a name to the numpy library called **np**. Any function from numpy carries the np prefix.

Chapter 5

Control Flow: While Loops

We often want computers to repeat steps until certain results are achieved. In those cases, we interrupt the flow by putting the code in a loop. There are two basic types of loops: **while** and **for**. I will start with while loops.

5.1 While Loops

While loops are written in block statements, the same way as the if statements. This rule also includes the colon mark at the end of the while line. In a while loop, Python will repeatedly check the condition specified by the coder. If True, it executes code in the block, which is indented by 4 spaces. If the condition returns False, it will exit the loop and bypass the block. It then resumes executing the code by the order of showing up.

Try this block of code

```
01 n = 0
02 while n <= 5:
03     print(n)
04     n = n + 1
```

Note that the condition in the block head changes because the variable **n** changes in each iteration. This is the major way of controlling the behavior of a while loop.

A convention often used by Python coders is to change line 4. $n = n + 1$ is often written as n += 1. You can extend this concept by having n += x, where x can be any number and is the incremental increase added to n.

Let's look at another example.

```
05 word = input("Give me a word: ")
06 while len(word) < 10:
07      word = word + "o"
08 print(word)
```

This block of code adds letter **o** to a word until it has ten characters.

5.2 Exit a While Loop

Your code will exit the loop when the condition is no longer true. Sometimes you want to break from the loop when some other condition is met. You can use the **break** command inside a loop. Try these lines:

```
09 n = 0
10 while True :
11      print(n)
12      n = n + 1
13      if n == 5 :
14          break
```

The **break** command will exit the code to the one immediate level up. In this case, it will exit the **while** loop. If you don't have the **break** command in the example above, the code will be stuck in an infinite loop.

If you prefer not to use **break**, you can have a switch on the condition. We can rewrite the previous example as:

```
15 n = 0
16 signal = True
17 while signal :
18      print(n)
19      n = n + 1
20      if n == 5 :
21          signal = False
```

5.3 Getting Stuck in a Loop

Sometimes a coder might paint himself into a corner and put the code in an infinite loop. For a novice, when the computer repeats itself, it is often a panic moment. You should be careful when writing a loop, but when the computer is stuck in a loop, it is not the end of the world. Spyder has a short-cut to get out of the infinite loop.

In the following graph, 1 points to a red square. It is the panic button you should push when you are stuck. Python will abruptly terminate any running code. This also works for any long procedure that you don't wish to continue.

Alternately, you can also go to **Consoles** (where 2 points in the graph) in the menu bar and select **Restart kennel** to interrupt the code and start over.

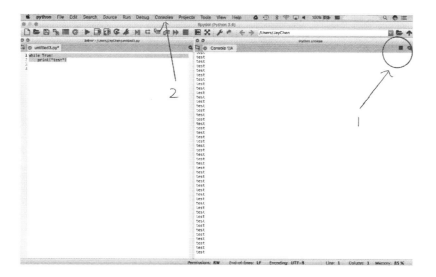

5.4 Unknown Rounds of Repetition

Loops are for repetitive work, but sometimes we cannot foresee the number of loops we need. When we interact with users, their behaviors are not always predictable. For example, in the history quiz example in Chapter 4, if the user keeps entering an answer not in the choice menu, the code will have to repeatedly ask the user to supply some answer that is recognizable. While loops are perfect for such cases.

We can rewrite the quiz example as

```
22 print("Which of the following was not a U.S. President?")
23 print("a. Alexander Hamilton")
24 print("b. George Washington")
25 print("c. John Adams")
26 print("d. Thomas Jefferson")
27
28 answer = input("Your answer is: ")
29
30 while answer not in "abcd":
31     print("Please only enter a, b, c, or d.")
32     answer = input("Your answer is: ")
33 if answer == "a":
34     print("Great. You are right.")
35 else:
36     print("I am sorry. You are wrong.")
```

5.5   Exercises

Questions with asterisks have sample solutions on the book's website
(www.csandaa.com/python-book).

1. Write a Python program to ask the user to find the square root of 81. If the user doesn't get the answer right, show the question again. It repeats until the user gets it right.

2. Write a Python program to ask a word from the user (ex. "Yellowstone") and print out
   #1 letter is Y
   #2 letter is e
   #3 letter is l
   :
   :

3.* The factorial of non-negative integer **n** is defined as

$$n! = n \times (n - 1) \times (n - 2) \times \cdots \times 2 \times 1.$$

Write a Python program with a while loop to find the factorial $n!$ with **n** given by the user. Note that the factorial can grow really fast. When you test the program, try using a smaller **n**. For example, $5! = 120$.

4.* Write a Python program to print out

0 seconds
5 seconds
10 seconds
⋮
⋮

Each line shows up at the interval of 5 seconds. A useful function **time.sleep( )** in the **time** library can stop the code temporarily by the number of seconds supplied in the argument. Make sure you do the following and use a while loop.

import time

Chapter 6

Control Flow: For Loops

Compared to **while** loops, **for** loops are a less restrictive and more powerful tool for repetitive work.

6.1   For Loops

Let's look at a problem that can be solved by both while and for loops. If we want to add the numbers from 1 to 100, we can use a while loop.

```
01 i = 1
02 sum = 0
03 while i <= 100 :
04     sum = sum + i
05     i += 1
06 print(sum)
```

The above is a typical while loop. As long as the variable **i** remains no more than 100, the loop continues. Also remember that line 5 is the same as i = i + 1.

A for loop is also a block statement. Python executes lines inside the block according to the specification in the first line of the block.

```
07 sum = 0
08 for i in range(101) :
09     sum = sum + i
10 print(sum)
```

The for loop looks more efficient than the while one, but the true power of the former is not about having fewer lines as shown. It is about known iteration steps. The while loop tests a condition and repeats the action if the condition is true, but the for loop explicitly repeats the number of iterations the coder asks for.

In this example, **i**, known as the counter or iterator, carries a value one at a time from the list **[0, 1, 2,.....,100]** (this is from range(101) and will be explained in the next section), in the order of the values in the list. Because iteration can be done over any sequence, for loops are therefore extremely flexible. Another example:

```
11 for i in "Python" :
12     print(i)
```

The output is

```
P
y
t
h
o
n
```

6.2   range( )

In line 8, I introduce the function **range( )** without much explanation. It is a major tool used in for loops and deserves a section of its own. Range( ) offers a quick way to generate a list that can be used in a for loop. If there is only one argument (parameter) supplied to the function, it will produce a list that starts from zero and ends right before the number. For example, **range(n)** produce a list **[0, 1, 2,....., n-1]**.

The idea behind range( ) is similar to indexing and slicing we see in lists and strings. We can also supply two arguments –**range(start, stop)**. The default incremental increase in range( ) is 1, but you can also change the step increase by supplying three arguments – **range(start, stop, step)**. For example, you can try in IPython Console

```
In    [1]: n = range(0, 100, 2)
In    [2]: n[20]
Out [2]: 40
```

Here, n is a list **[0, 2, 4,..., 96, 98]** and its 21st element is number 40.

IPython Console suppresses the output of the list generated from range( ) because Python calls it a range object. But it is a bona-fide list in the computer memory. You treat it and use it the same way you do to a list. Note that all the arguments must be integers, but can be negative, if necessary. For example, you can create a list with **range(100, 0, -1)**.

Combining range( ) and len( ) is frequently seen in data processing. Instead of iterating over the sequence, we can use the order of the sequence for the iteration.

```
13 text = "Python"
14 for i in range(len(text)):
15     print(text[i])
```

Line 13-15 don't look as elegant as line 11-12, but they deliver the same result. There are occasions where less elegant solutions are useful. Having options is always a good thing.

6.3   The Iterator

The iterator is the variable that sequentially takes values in the sequence in the block head. But it doesn't have to be in the block of code. For example, the following code prints out "Python" a hundred times.

```
16 for i in range(100):
17     print("Python")
```

But those occasions are rare. Iterators themselves are useful.

6.4   Exercises

Questions with asterisks have sample solutions on the book's website (www.csandaa.com/python-book).

1. Use range( ) and a for loop to generate a list [**0, 0.1, 0.2,......, 0.99**].

2. Redo the following exercise from Chapter 5, but use a for loop instead: Write a Python program to ask a word from the user (ex. "Yellowstone") and print out
   #1 letter is Y
   #2 letter is e
   #3 letter is l
   :

:

3.* **N** is a list: [1, 4, 7, 9, 13, 26, 48, 206, 509, 1218]. Write a Python program to print out a new list populated with only odd numbers from **N**.

4. String objects have a **.lower( )** method that can covert upper-case letters to lower-case ones. Write a Python program to convert a string from the user input to all lower-case letters. Your program should also drop non-alphabet characters.

5.* Redo Exercise 4 of Chapter 5 with a for loop. Write a Python program to print out
    0 seconds
    5 seconds
    10 seconds
    :
    :
    Each line shows up at the interval of 5 seconds. A useful function **time.sleep( )** in the **time** library can stop the code temporarily by the number of seconds supplied in the argument.

6.* Ask the user for two text strings. Write a Python program to print out a list populated with only common letters in the two strings.

7. Write a Python program with a for loop to find the factorial $n!$ with **n** given by the user.

8. A deck of poker has 52 cards. They are divided into 4 suits: Spade (S), Heart (H), Diamond (D), and Club (C). Each suit has 13 ranks: A, 2, 3, 4, 5, 6, 7, 8, 9, 10, J, Q, and K. Use a nested for loop to create a list of all 52 cards denoted with their suit and rank, e.g. "S4". Then import from the numpy library **np.random.choice( )** function to randomly draw a card. Print out the card drawing result.

9. Write a Python program to determine whether an integer is a prime number.

10.* [**1, 1, 2, 3, 5, 8, 13, 21, 34, 55,...**] is an infinite series. Each item, except the first two, takes value the sum of the previous two numbers. What is **nth** item's value?

11. Find the max value in a list using the placeholder algorithm. You are asked to generate a random list of 1,000 numbers. Write a Python program to find the largest of the list. To generate a list of random numbers, you use

    import random
    rand_list = random.randint(0, 1000)

Note that **(0, 1000)** are the low and high values of the possible drawings for the **randint( )** function. And the function only draws one number at a time. You need to use a for loop to populate the list.

12. Caesar Cipher revisit. Redo the same exercise in Chapter 3, but you do not limit the length of the message.

Chapter 7

Financial Application: Monte Carlo Simulations

Now that we have enough knowledge about Python basics, we can have our first Python application in finance. Finance practitioners deal with uncertainties on a daily basis. Stock prices are known to be unpredictable, yet the entire profession is based on managing the unpredictable.

For example, a young man who just got his paycheck is ready to open a retirement account. What should he buy? How likely is the money that he invests in the account going to grow over time? At what rate? Or if a company is ready to acquire a rival, what is the price to pay for the target company? How likely the acquisition will lead to strategic synergy? Or when a pension fund has a load of U.S. Treasury bond, what does the Fed's new policy mean for their holdings? What should they do? Increase, decrease, or just re-balance? Lots of unknowns.

One way to manage the unknowns is to run a Monte Carlo simulation. But what is it? A Monte Carlo simulation does not have deterministic views of the future. Instead, it lets the future play out a million times, or, if you like, hundreds of millions times. Then you analyze the distribution of these simulated futures. In a nut shell, Monte Carlo simulations use random drawings from a predetermined probability distribution to forecast the outcome of a random event.

7.1 Throwing a Dice

We can run a Monte Carlo simulation to forecast the outcome of throwing a fair dice. Try these lines:

```
01 import random
02 result=[ ]
03 count = 0
04 for i in range(1000):
05     face = random.randint(1, 6)
06     result.append(face)
07     if face == 6:
08         count += 1
09 print(count/len(result))
```

In the script above, **random.randint( )** draws one integer between the two values (included) in the arguments supplied. So code in lines 1-9 produces the simulated probability of the dice showing **6**. You just have one assumption, faces 1 to 6 are equally likely to turn up. The function random.randint( ) draws the outcome from a uniform distribution.

The dice example seems to be an overkill because you intuitively know a fair dice has such a probability. But what if "playing out" the future is not as simple as throwing a dice?

7.2   Wealth Accumulation

In real life, random events are less likely to follow a uniform distribution like dice-throwing. Many events follow a normal distribution or can be approximated by it. In that case, we use **random.gauss(mean, sigma)**, where **mean** is the mean of the underlying normal distribution and **sigma** its standard deviation.

Let's look at a problem in portfolio management for a financial adviser. If you want to find out for your client how much wealth she could accumulate after 30 years of saving $500 per month, you could take the cash flows and apply the mean monthly return of the stock market to the savings. That gives you **one** possible future. In fact, you know that future has zero chance of realization, if you have some idea of probability theory.

Monte Carlo simulations answer the question differently. What is a normal investment's monthly return on average? How much variation do these investment returns have? The mean and the standard deviation, the measure for variation, constitute a normal distribution. Instead of assuming the investor can get the mean return regularly, why don't we just draw a possible return from the return distribution? If we do it for 360 months, we can have a future for the client. If we repeat 1 million times, we can have 1 million futures for her. Then we can infer from the million outcomes and offer our recommendation. This procedure is implemented in the following code.

```
10 import random
11 import numpy as np
11 wealth = [ ]
12 for i in range(1000000):
13      ending = 0
14      for j in range(360):
15          ending = 500 + ending*(1+ random.gauss(0.008, 0.015))
16      wealth.append(ending)
17 np.mean(wealth)
```

Once you run the code, you will see a number close to $1 million dollars. All the million "futures" are stored in the list **wealth**. And the printed outcome is the average of the futures, calculated by the function **np.mean( )**. Later in Chapter 9, we will learn how to plot a histogram based on a list such as wealth here. Since *a picture is worth a thousand words*, You can convince your client more easily with a nice distribution printout.

Depending on your settings, Monte Carlo simulations can take a long period of time to finish. Since you are running the simulation with 1 million iterations, it will take some time to get the result. Coders often try with fewer iterations first to make sure the code is correctly constructed. That is a good tip.

In this simulation, we assume the client's saving is put into an investment that returns .8% per month with return standard deviation of 1.5%. The function **random.gauss(μ, σ)** is to draw an outcome from a normal distribution with a given mean μ and a standard deviation σ. So line 15 is to increase her monthly balance by the sum of the new savings of $500 and the net return of her previous balance.

See if you can use Excel to implement the same algorithm. If you are used to spreadsheet-based number crunching, this will probably be the first time you are awed by the power of a programming language.

7.3 Exercises

Questions with asterisks have sample solutions on the book's website (www.csandaa.com/python-book).

1.* Write a Python program to run a Monte Carlo simulation to find out the probability of having a **pair** when drawing two cards from a deck of Poker cards. A pair of cards is defined as two cards with the same rank.

2. When drawing five cards from a deck, there are ranks among the possible combinations. For example, **Four of a Kind**, a hand containing all four cards of the same

rank, trumps **Full House**, a hand with a Three of a Kind and a Pair. The ranks are based on the occurrence probability. Harder-to-get hands are ranked higher. To save time, you can copy and paste the complete card list you did in Exercise 8 of Chapter 6.

Write a Python program to run a Monte Carlo simulation to show why **Flush**, defined as any five cards of the same suit, beats **Straight**, defined as five cards in sequence of mixed suits. Also use the list generated in Exercise of Chapter 6.

3.* Roulette is a casino game in which the player bets on where the ball falls in a spinning wheel. American roulette has numbers from 1 to 36, plus the obnoxious 0 and 00. The wheel is fair and the ball has an equal chance of falling into any of these 38 number pockets. If you bet on any individual number and win, the payoff is 36:1, meaning your $1 bet will return as $36 ($35 is the winning and $1 your original bet).

Let's run a Monte Carlo Simulation to understand how terrible the odds are for the player. Write a Python program to complete the following task:

Draw 1,000,000 random integer numbers between 0 and 37, using the function random.randint(0, 37). We use 37 to represent 00. Collect these random numbers in a list. Find the number of occurrences of the number 1 in your list. If you bet $5 on a number for 1,000,000 times, find out the total amount of loss.

The moral of this exercise is that the longer you sit at a roulette table, the more likely the house will take you to the cleaner. If your result doesn't show that, your program is wrong.

4. Bill Gates vs. Casino. A gambler can also bet on whether the roulette number is odd or even. Since 0 and 00 don't count, the odd to win is not 2:1, but the payoff is only 2:1. The payoff includes one's own bet. Given this unfavorable odd, a gambler with a deep pocket, such as Bill Gates, can still beat the house if he follows a strict double-down routine. In such routine, the gambler doubles down when he loses. If he wins, he recovers all previous losses with some more. He then returns to his original bet size.

Write a Python program to calculate how deep the gambler's pocket must have, if each bet is $5, to guarantee a winning day.

5.* SPY. SPY, officially known as the SPDR® S&P 500® ETF Trust, is an exchange-traded fund run by State Street Global Advisers to track the performance of the S&P 500® Index. It is shown to have .82% monthly return with a standard deviation of 4.22%. You will do the same exercise as in Section 7.2 to find out the wealth after accumulating for 30 years in SPY.

Since it will take some time for Python to run 1 million times for this, I suggest you start with 1,000 times to make sure everything works alright.

Collect all 1 million possible wealth paths in a list. Report the mean and standard deviation of these ending wealth balances. You need to import **numpy** library and two functions **np.mean( )** and **np.std( )**. What do these numbers tell you?

Chapter 8

User-Defined Functions

Coding so far feels like running through a series of steps. It is indeed similar to a production line in a factory. You move a line or two down the conveyor belt and Python will process them. But what if we can have prefabricated blocks, like Legos, in the production line? This is called modularization. It is a widely used method for efficient manufacturing. It is also critical in coding. Modularization not only allows for repetitive use of code, but also makes maintenance of code a much easier job.

8.1 Functions as a Block

The built-in functions and those imported from various libraries are also Python code. We use them without knowing the parts inside. You throw arguments in the functions and they return things that we need. But these built-in functions are not customizable. Coders can have a very specific need and therefore want to write their own functions.

A user-defined function starts just like all other block statements. Try these lines:

```
01 def Fahrenheit(C):
02     F = 32 + C*9/5
03     return F
04 print(Fahrenheit(100))
```

def starts the function block, the same way as **if**, **while** and **for**. You also end the first line with the colon mark and indent 4 spaces (1 tab) for the ensuing lines. **Fahrenheit(C)** here gives your user-defined function a name called **Fahrenheit( )**. You use it just the same way as you use any external function. The argument (also known as a parameter or an input) **C** is given by the function caller and its value is passed to the variable inside the block statement. Such variable(s) are local to the function and unrecognizable outside of it.

At the end of a user-defined function, we would typically return one or more values. These outputs are the reasons why we have black box-like functions. If this is a bit confusing, try to compare a user-defined function to a built-in one. For example, the built-in len( ) takes in a sequence as an argument and returns the length of the sequence. You can picture the len( ) function as having the following pseudo-code:

```
05 def len(sequence):
06      length = (the length of sequence) #This part is not real Python code.
07      return length
```

The analogy should help you with the concept of a user-defined function. If you don't return anything, Python will automatically assign **None** as the return value of your function.

8.2   User-Defined Functions as Modules

Of course, you don't have to use user-defined functions to code. Some beginners even dislike user-defined functions' extra layer of complexitiy. But you will see the power of these functions after you modularize your work. Here is an example of modularization.

Suppose you want to create a table listing temperatures in Celsius and their corresponding Fahrenheit degrees. You can call your user-defined function repeatedly for the job.

```
08 def Fahrenheit(C):
09      F = 32 + C*9/5
10      return F
11 for i in range(101):
12      print("Celsius: ", i, "; Fahrenheit: ", Fahrenheit(i))
```

Later on, when we tackle a harder problem, we will break it into pieces of smaller problems. We will then see the full power of modularization. Exercise 5 of this chapter gives you a glimpse of modularized coding. A coder joke says, "Once you finish defining all your functions, you are done with your code."

8.3   Exercises

Questions with asterisks have sample solutions on the book's website (www.csandaa.com/python-book).

1.* Write a user-defined Python function **my_sum(n)** to find the running sum of the first **n** natural numbers.

2. Write a user-defined Python function **factorial(n)** to find factorial of a given number **n**.

3.* Write a user-defined Python function **my_max(x)** to find the maximum value of a list **x** of numbers, using the placeholder algorithm.

4. Write a user-defined Python function **quadratic(a, b, c)** to solve for a quadratic equation. The function should take three inputs as the three coefficients of the equation and return the two roots. If there are no real roots, return a message saying, "No real roots."

   The formula for a quadratic equation roots: For $ax^2 + bx + c = 0$, $x = \dfrac{-b \pm \sqrt{b^2 - 4ac}}{2a}$.

5. The Monte Carlo simulation we did in Exercises 1 and 2 of Chapter 7 can be more efficiently done with user-defined functions.

   (a) A poker hand. Write a user-defined function to draw a 5-card hand from a deck of cards. Use the list (with its notations) we generated in Exercise 8 of Chapter 6. The function takes no arguments and the result returned is a nested list, e.g. [["S", "3"], ["D", "K"], ["D", "2"], ["H", "9"], ["H", "3"]].
   Note: Using "T" to replace "10" can be productive.

   (b) Is the hand a **Straight Flush**? A Straight Flush has 5 sequential ranks of the same suit. AKQJT and 5432A are both Straights. Write a user-defined function to determine whether a hand is a Straight Flush. Return True it if is and False if not. The input argument is the hand you generate in part (a).

   (c) Is the hand a **Four of a Kind**? A Four of a Kind has all 4 suits of the same rank. Write a user-defined function to determine whether a hand is a Four of a Kind. Return True it if is and False if not. The input argument is the hand you generate in part (a).

   (d) Is the hand a **Full House**? A Full House has three cards of the same rank and two of another. Write a user-defined function to determine whether a hand is a Full House. Return True it if is and False if not. The input argument is the hand you generate in part (a).

   (e) Is the hand a **Flush**? A Flush has all five cards of the same suit, but is not a Straight Flush. Write a user-defined function to determine whether a hand is a Flush. Return True it if is and False if not. The input argument is the hand you generate in part (a). In your function, you should call the Straight Flush function and make sure it returns False.

(f)* Is the hand a **Straight**? A Straight has five sequential ranks, but is not a Straight Flush. Write a user-defined function to determine whether a hand is a Straight. Return True it if is and False if not. The input argument is the hand you generate in part (a). In your function, you should call the Straight Flush function and make sure it returns False.

(g)* Is the hand a **Three of a Kind**? A Three of a Kind has three cards of the same rank, but is not a Full House. Write a user-defined function to determine whether a hand is a Three of a Kind. Return True it if is and False if not. The input argument is the hand you generate in part (a). In your function, you should call the Full House function and make sure it returns False.

(h) Is the hand a **Two Pair**? A Two Pair has two sets of pairs (two cards of the same rank), but is not a Full House. Write a user-defined function to determine whether a hand is a Three of a Kind. Return True it if is and False if not. The input argument is the hand you generate in part (a). In your function, you should call the Full House function and make sure it returns False.

(i) Is the hand a **One Pair**? A One Pair two cards of the same rank, but is not a Four of a Kind, Three of a Kind, Two Pair, or a Full House. Write a user-defined function to determine whether a hand is a One Pair. Return True it if is and False if not. The input argument is the hand you generate in part (a). In your function, you should call the Four of a Kind, Three of a Kind, Two Pair, and Full House functions and make sure they all return False.

(j) Redo Exercises 1 and 2 of Chapter 7.

6. Bond pricing. Bonds can be priced according to the following formula:

$$Price = \frac{Coupon_1}{1 + \frac{YTM}{2}} + \frac{Coupon_2}{(1 + \frac{YTM}{2})^2} + \frac{Coupon_3}{(1 + \frac{YTM}{2})^3} + \ldots\ldots + \frac{Coupon_{2T} + Par}{(1 + \frac{YTM}{2})^{2T}},$$

where $Coupon_n$ is the nth semi-annual coupon payment, YTM the yield to maturity, and Par the face value of the bond (typically \$1,000), and T the number of years to maturity.

Write a user-defined Python function **bond(CR, YTM, T)** to determine a bond's price.

7.* The Efficient Frontier. With asset return r and standard deviation σ, we can describe a two-asset portfolio as:

$$r_p = x_a r_a + x_b r_b;$$
$$\sigma_p^2 = x_a^2 \sigma_a^2 + x_b^2 \sigma_b^2 + 2x_a x_b \sigma_a \sigma_b \rho_{ab},$$

where ρ_{ab} is the correlation coefficient between assets a and b.

(a) Write a user-defined Python function **portfolio(xa, xb, ra, rb, sig_a, sig_b, rho)** to produce a portfolio's return and standard deviation.

(b) In the last ten years, SPY has a monthly return of .0064 and standard deviation of .044; BND has a monthly return of .0034 and standard deviation of .011. The two ETFs have a correlation coefficient of .0188. Use the two ETFs to create 100 portfolios. Pick the best one out of the 100. Explain your pick.

Chapter 9

Plotting

Data is sometimes hard to visualize and understand. What can better visualize data than a graph? Python has powerful libraries for plotting purposes.

Computers plot in a different way than humans. They show pixels in assigned locations on a 2D plane or a 3D space. With perfect aligned locations of pixels and colors, computers can draw any graph a human can create. What matters now is how to supply the right locations on the graph for those pixels to show up.

9.1   X-Y Scatter Plot

The most common graph is the x-y scatter plot. An x-y scatter plot is an example of using Cartesian coordinates to draw a graph. Try these lines.

```
01 import matplotlib.pyplot as plt
02 x = [1, 2, 3]
03 y = [3, 2, 1]
04 plt.plot(x, y)
```

The library **matplotlib.pyplot** is the main plotting tool in Python. It has its roots in MatLab®. We will use it a lot from now on. Here I first establish all the coordinates of x's and y's. Specifically, we are plotting a line connecting three points—(1, 3), (2, 2), and (3, 1). The function plt.plot( ) always draws a line by connecting successive points. If you don't like the default, try changing to other styles with options provided in the next section.

9.2   Color and Line Type

plt.plot( ) can take an optional third argument to change the color and type of the points you lay on the graph. For example, **plt.plot(x, y, 'ro')** changes the default color to red and the default marker from a line to a circle.

Here is a list of commonly used colors:

"b": blue
"g": green
"r": red
"c": cyan
"m": magenta
"y": yellow
"k": black
"w": white

Here is a list of selected marker types:

".": point
",": pixel
"o": circle
"v": triangle down
"8": octagon
"s": square
"p": pentagon
"P": plus (filled)
"*": star
"h": hexagon1
"H": hexagon2
"+": plus
"x": x
"X": x (filled)
"D": diamond
"d": thin diamond
"—": vline
"_": hline

9.3 Histogram

The library matplotlib.pyplot can do way more than scatter plots. We will learn some more in the future chapters. For now, let's look at one widely used statistical plot—a histogram.

```
05 import matplotlib.pyplot as plt
06 import random
07 x=[ ]
08 for i in range(1000):
09       x.append(random.gauss(.0082, .0422))
10 plt.hist(x, 50, facecolor='b', alpha=0.5)
```

In the code above, I draw 1,000 monthly returns from a normal distribution with a mean of .0082 and a standard deviation of .0422. This distribution is similar to the U.S. stock market performance.

plt.hist( ) takes four arguments. The first is the data, which is in a list. The three extra arguments are the number of bins, the face color of the histogram, and transparency of the graph, respectively. **alpha** is between 0 and 1, with 1 being the most opaque. Try changing the arguments to see the effects.

9.4 Labeling and Other Settings

Spyder's graphic output is shown in IPython Console. If you plot two graphs successively, the second one will replace the first. If you want to see two seperate graphs, you will have to initiate a new graph with the function **plt.figure( )**. The following code also includes a few useful plotting functions. Brief explanations are written after the hashtag.

```
11 import matplotlib.pyplot as plt
12 x = [1, 2, 3]
13 y = [3, 2, 1]
14 plt.plot(x, y, "ro")
15
16 plt.figure( )
17
18 x = [1, 2, 3]
19 y = [40, 98, 76]
20 plt.plot(x, y, "bo")
21 plt.title("Finance Test") #Give the graph a title.
22 plt.xlabel("Student") #Label x-axis.
23 plt.ylabel("Score") #Label y-axis.
```

24 **plt.xticks([1, 2, 3], ['Adam', 'Ben', 'Carlos'])** #Replace x-axis ticks.
25 **plt.ylim([0, 100])** #Set y-axis limits.
26 **plt.grid( )** #Draw grid lines.

9.5   Exercises

Questions with asterisks have sample solutions on the book's website
(www.csandaa.com/python-book).

1.* Write a Python program to draw the number **2**. You should first draw the number on
a piece of graph paper. You then look at your 2 on paper and pick out some points
on it. You should record the coordinates of these points you pick out and enter them
into two lists. The more points you have on the paper, the smoother a line you will
get.

2. The Efficient Frontier. Plot the frontier you created in Exercise 7.b of Chapter 8. You
should plot r_p against σ_p.

3. Outliers. You've got a list of historical prices for a certain stock. Download the data
from the book website to your working directory. Unfortunately, the list includes an
erroneously inserted outlier. Report the position and value of the outlier. Pop the
outlier from the list. Plot it.

4.* Semi-circles. A semi-circle takes the function $y = \sqrt{r^2 - x^2}$, where r is the radius.
Write a Python program to draw a semi-circle with a radius of 10.

5. A stock chart. A stock's monthly closing prices in one year are in the following table.
Plot a time series with the settings learned in 9.4.

Month	Closing Price
January	108
February	104
March	143
April	144
May	162
June	169
July	178
August	206
September	211
October	193
November	245
December	228

6. Random walk. Write a Python program to plot a stock price series that follows a random walk. The stock in the beginning trades at \$100 per share. Its monthly return is .82% with a standard deviation of 4.22%. You will draw a random monthly return from such a distribution for 360 months. Plot a stock series with such returns. Does the series look like any market index?

Chapter 10

Numerical Methods

When we have a math problem that doesn't have a perfect analytic solution or the analytic solution is hard to find, we turn to computers for a numerical solution. The idea behind numerical methods is to use the computers' ability to repeatedly try various answers and find the ones that approximate the real solutions.

10.1   Cubic Roots

What is the cubic root of any real number? We can start by guessing a number as its potential root and then take that number to the third power and see how close it is to the real number. Try these:

```
01 def cubic(n):
02      guess = 0
03      while guess <= n:
04          if guess**3 >= n:
05              break
06          guess += 1 #incremental increase
07      return guess
08 cubic(125)
```

Here are some explanations for the code above. To find the cubic root of a number, I try to guess an answer and then take it to the third power. If the third power has not exceeded the number in question, I increase the guessed answer by some incremental value. The process repeats until the guessed answer has a cube greater than the number.

Since it is written in a user-defined function, it can be used to find any number's cubic root in theory.

There are two important numbers in numerical methods as you see in the above example. The first is the initial value (**guess = 0**) of the approximation process. Starting the initial value as a small number increases the chance of covering all possibilities, but potentially wastes your computer power. It is a balancing act.

The same is true for the second number, the incremental increase in the iteration process. A larger increase saves time and computing power, while a smaller one gives you higher accuracy. Try **cubic(126)** with the same script. You will see that an incremental increase of 1 is too inaccurate. You can change the line **guess += 1** to **guess += .1** to see the effect.

10.2   Quadratic Equations

For the quadratic equation $ax^2 + bx + c = 0$, we can apply the formula $x = \dfrac{-b \pm \sqrt{b^2 - 4ac}}{2a}$ for the roots. It has a clear analytic solution. But to help us understand the numerical methods, we can try to solve the quadratic equation with the numerical method.

For example, a quadratic equation $x^2 - 3x + 2 = 0$ has two roots. They are in fact the intersections of two lines on the Cartesian plane: $y = x^2 - 3x + 2$ and $y = 0$, as you can see in the following graph.

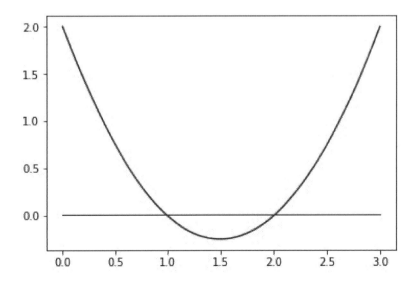

To find the intersections numerically, we can guess the roots (**x's**) and test whether those guesses produce **y's** that are close enough to the horizontal x-axis. Try these lines.

```
09 import matplotlib.pyplot as plt
10
11 def curve(x):
12      y = x**2 - 3*x + 2
13      return y
14
15 x = [ ] #Create lists to store trial point coordinates and roots.
16 y = [ ]
17 roots = [ ]
18
19 for i in range(300):
20      x.append(i/100)
21      y.append(curve(i/100))
22      if curve(i/100) == 0:
23          roots.append(i/100)
24
25 plt.plot(x,y)
26 print("Roots are ", roots)
```

In the code, I plot 300 points, as you see in the for loop. But the 300 points are squeezed in between $x = 0$ and $x = 2.99$. Therefore, the incremental increase is .01 and the initial guess is 0. We are lucky that the trials are perfect intersections of the two curves. That is rarely the case in reality.

Let's look at another example: Solve numerically the quadratic equation $x^2 + 5x + 2 = 0$.

```
27 import matplotlib.pyplot as plt
28
29 def curve(x):
30      y = x**2 + 5*x + 2
31      return y
32
33 x = [ ] #Create lists to store trial point coordinates and roots.
34 y = [ ]
35 z = [ ]
36 roots = [ ]
37
38 for i in range(-600,200): #The range is based on some trials and errors.
```

```
39        x.append(i/100)
40        y.append(curve(i/100))
41        z.append(0) # (x, z) is to plot the flat x-axis.
42        if curve(i/100)*curve((i-1)/100) <= 0:
43            roots.append(i/100)
44
45 plt.plot(x, y)
46 plt.plot(x,vz)
47 print("Roots are ", roots)
```

The trick in line 42 is that when the parabola crosses the x-axis, the sign of $y's$ changes. The product of two successive $y's$ will briefly change from positive to negative. I select the points as the roots right before the sign changes. You can of course pick the points that are right after the changes. Since they are numerical, not exact, solutions, the difference is not significant.

10.3   Exercises

Questions with asterisks have sample solutions on the book's website (www.csandaa.com/python-book).

1.* Rewrite the cubic root example to accommodate a negative real number.

2. A third power polynomial function. Write a Python program to numerically solve $x^3 + 2x^2 - 6x + 2 = 0$. Note that there are three roots for this polynomial function.

3.* Approximation of π. A circle with radius r can be stuffed inside a $2r \times 2r$ square. Since a circle's area is πr^2 and said square's $4r^2$, the area ratio of the circle to the square is $\frac{\pi}{4}$. We can use this fact and Monte Carlo simulations to find the approximation of π.

   (a) Let's focus on the top-right quadrant. Use **random.randint( )** from the **random** library to pick points on a Cartesian plane between (0, 0) and (1,000,000, 1,000,000). You can start with 1 million points and increase the magnitude of order to see the effect.

   (b) For each randomly picked point, test whether it is inside the circle or outside of it. Remember a semi-circle's function is $y = \sqrt{r^2 - x^2}$. Therefore, if your point (x_i, y_i) is such that $x_i^2 + y_i^2 \leqslant r^2$, it is inside the circle.

   (c) Record the number of points that are inside the circle. Divide it by the total number of points picked. The ratio is then $\frac{\pi}{4}$. Report your π approximation. If you add more points, you will get even more accurate π.

4. Internal rate of return (IRR). A five-year auto loan is typically amortized on a monthly basis. Write a Python program to determine the interest rate on a $38,000 loan that requires a monthly payment of $690.

   Note that nominal interest rates in theory have a lower bound of zero. They rarely go beyond 20% lately. Use these hints to form your guesses.

5. The bond yield. Write a Python program to find the yield to maturity of a bond that sells for $980 with a coupon rate of 0.5%. The bond just paid a semi-annual coupon and will mature in 2 years. Recall the bond pricing formula is

$$Price = \frac{Coupon_1}{1 + \frac{YTM}{2}} + \frac{Coupon_2}{(1 + \frac{YTM}{2})^2} + \frac{Coupon_3}{(1 + \frac{YTM}{2})^3} + \ldots\ldots + \frac{Coupon_{2T} + Par}{(1 + \frac{YTM}{2})^{2T}},$$

   where $Coupon_n$ is the nth semi-annual coupon payment, YTM the yield to maturity, and Par the face value of the bond (typically $1,000), and T the number of years to maturity.

6.* Option pricing and implied volatility. Beyond the variations of dividend discount models, equity pricing used to be known as wildly inaccurate. It finally gained mathematical sophistication after Fischer Black and Myron Scholes published the seminal work on option pricing (Black and Scholes, 1973).

   The Black-Scholes Model shows that there are only six factors that determine an option's price: the underlying stock's current price, the option's strike (exercise) price, the risk-free interest rate, the stock's volatility measured in return standard deviations, the option contract's time to expiration, and the stock's dividend payout.

   A call option of a stock that doesn't pay dividends can be priced according to the Black-Scholes Model:

   $C = S_0 N(d_1) - Xe^{-Rt} N(d_2)$, where

   $d_1 = \frac{\ln(S_0/X) + (R + \sigma^2/2)t}{\sqrt{\sigma^2 t}}$;

   $d_2 = d_1 - \sqrt{\sigma^2 t}$.

   The parameters of the Black-Scholes Model are

   S_0 : current stock price

X : strike price

R : annual risk-free rate, continuously compounded

σ : standard deviation (per year) of stock return

t : time to maturity (in years)

$N(d)$: probability that a standardized, normally distributed random variable will be less than d

(a)* Write a user-defined function **call(S, X, R, sigma, t)** to price call options. Note that to calculate the natural logarithm, you need to import the library **numpy** to use the function **np.log( )**. To find the exponent of **e**, use **np.exp( )**.

To calculate $N(d_1)$ and $N(d_2)$, you will need the **norm.cdf( )** function from the **scipy.stats** library. Specifically,

from scipy.stats import norm
norm.cdf(d, loc— , scale—)

You need to supply a number after loc= for the mean, scale= for the standard deviation. In this problem, the distribution is standard normal. Therefore, loc = 0 and scale = 1.

(b)* Implied volatility is a calculated σ. If we know a call option's value, we can deduce its implied volatility. Find the implied volatility for the following call option: 470 days to expiration, interest rate 1%, stock price \$350, strike price \$500, and option value \$18.

The famous **VIX**, volatility index, is calculated in the fashion of implied volatility. The options on the S&P 500® Index are publicly traded. Since the option prices are known, implied volatility can be deducted from the Black-Scholes Model. This volatility measure itself becomes something tradable. It even has its own derivatives!

(c) Challenge. Write a user-defined Python function to compute implied volatility of any call option.

(d) More challenge—volatility smile. Go to an online source, such as Google Finance or Yahoo Finance, to get a series of call option prices of a stock traded in the

U.S. Find their implied volatility and plot implied volatility against strike prices. Do you see a smile or a smirk?

Chapter 11

Pandas: Data Structure

This is the first chapter we learn about the **Pandas** library. Pandas was created by Wes McKinney to deal with multidimensional data. McKinney's original Pandas book (McKinney, 2012) might be somehow outdated, but still a good starting text for Pandas. As an ever-enlarging, open-sourced library of functions, Pandas gives Python such powerful tools that it is now considered as one of the two main data analysis languages, with the other one being **R**.

11.1 DataFrame

Excel popularizes the concept of a spreadsheet. It is now convenient to view data in the format of a spreadsheet. Pandas's **DataFrame** object is to turn data into a spreadsheet-like structure.

Go to the book's website to download NASDAQCOM.csv[1]. Save it to the working directory where you use your Spyder. You can change the working directory from the top right corner of the Spyder window. It is a good practice to store all the data files and your working .py file in the same working directory.

Then try the following lines. If there is a **FileNotFound** error, try to include in the function argument the full directory path, not just the .csv file name. This appears to be a common problem among Mac users.

```
01 import pandas as pd
02 data = pd.read_csv('NASDAQCOM.csv')
```

---

[1]Data is from Nasdaq OMX Group through Fred2 database maintained by Federal Reserve Bank of St. Louis.

The function **read_csv( )** is to read an external data file. The .csv file type is the most commonly used. Let's use IPython Console to take a look at the data you just imported.

```
In   [1]: data.head( )
Out [1]:
          DATE    NASDAQCOM
   0    2/5/1971          100
   1    2/8/1971       100.84
   2    2/9/1971       100.76
   3   2/10/1971       100.69
   4   2/11/1971       101.45
```

Once a .csv file is imported and assigned to a variable, the variable is recognized as a DataFrame object. It has many useful methods. The method **.head( )** provides the first five rows of data. You can peek more by supplying to the function the number of rows you want to see. From the head view, we see a data layout just like a spreadsheet. Note that Pandas automatically creates an index column for you. The index also starts from zero.

With the spreadsheet-concept in mind, you can call any specific cell by using the **.iloc** indexing method.

```
In   [2]: data.iloc[3, 1]
Out [2]: '100.69'
```

The **.iloc** indexing method calls elements by their relative positions (locations) in the data, but you can also call call an entire column by its header.

```
In   [3]: data1 = data['NASDAQCOM']
In   [4]: data1.head( )
Out [4]:
   0       100
   1    100.84
   2    100.76
   3    100.69
   4    101.45
Name: NASDAQCOM, dtype: object
```

Because **data1** now is reduced to having one column, it becomes a different data type called **Series**, but it is very similar to DataFrame. Slicing and dicing on DataFrame or Series is done in the same way as lists. For example,

In [5]: data['NASDAQCOM'][0:2]
Out [5]:
0   100
1   100.84
Name: NASDAQCOM, dtype: object

In [6]: data.iloc[0:2, 1]
Out [6]:
0   100
1   100.84
Name: NASDAQCOM, dtype: object

If you call a column that doesn't match any existing header, you are creating a new column. But you have to assign values to it first. For example,

In [7]: data['Return'] = 0
In [8]: data.head( )
Out [8]:

	DATE	NASDAQCOM	Return
0	2/5/1971	100	0
1	2/8/1971	100.84	0
2	2/9/1971	100.76	0
3	2/10/1971	100.69	0
4	2/11/1971	101.45	0

11.2   Data Cleanup

DataFrame, just like lists, can have mixed types. We don't always know the types from the look of the data. But we can check.

In [9]: type(data['NASDAQCOM'])
Out [9]: pandas.core.series.Series

In [10]: type(data.iloc[100, 1])
Out [10]: str

The data series turns out to be a bunch of text strings, which don't allow math operations. It will be a problem, for example, if we want to turn a price series into a return one. In this file, it is worse because it has missing values (represented by "." in the data). The missing values are most likely the results of market's being closed. Here is the code to convert strings to numbers and remove missing values.

```
03 data = pd.read_csv('NASDAQCOM.csv', index_col=0)
04 data = data[data["NASDAQCOM"] != "."]
05 for i in range(len(data)):
06     data.iloc[i, 0] = float(data.iloc[i, 0])
```

Note that we add one more argument to **pd.read_csv( )** to make the date column to be the index column. This change can keep the index in order when we drop missing values. Once a column is designated as the index, it is not counted in the **.iloc** method. More on index in the next section.

```
In   [11]: data.head( )
Out [11]:
              NASDAQCOM
DATE
2/5/1971           100
2/8/1971        100.84
2/9/1971        100.76
2/10/1971       100.69
2/11/1971       101.45
```

Also in line 4, I did an implicit logical test inside the first square bracket of the data variable. By doing so, I exclude all the rows with missing values. In line 5, I use len(data). The length of a DataFrame object is the number of rows, excluding the header.

Sometimes, a dataset comes in with cells that are denoted as **N/A** or similar marks. Pandas can drop all these not-available data points by

```
In   [12]: data = data.dropna( )
```

11.3   DataFrame Index

The introduction of an index column has many benefits. Slicing data by labels is one of them. The method used for index label slicing is **.loc**.

```
In   [13]: data['Return'] = 0
In   [14]: data.loc['2/5/1971' : '2/9/1971']
Out [14]:
              NASDAQCOM    Return
     DATE
     2/5/1971              100        0
     2/8/1971           100.84        0
     2/9/1971           100.76        0
```

The .loc method is slightly different from ordinary Python slicing. In the arguments of .loc(start : end), **end** is included.

Label slicing can be applied to columns as well.

```
In   [15]: data.loc['2/5/1971' : '2/9/1971', "NASDAQCOM"]
Out [15]:
     DATE
     2/5/1971      100
     2/8/1971   100.84
     2/9/1971   100.76
Name: NASDAQCOM, dtype: object
```

Whether you use .loc or .iloc method, there is a quick trick to reverse the whole DataFrame.

```
In   [16]: data.loc[::-1]
Out [16]:
              NASDAQCOM    Return
     DATE
     10/3/2017          16531.71       0
     10/2/2017           6516.72       0
     9/29/2017           6495.96       0
     :                       :         :
```

The data used to have the oldest on top but now the latest is on top. The syntax inside .loc( ) or .iloc( ) is **.loc[start stop skip]**. **:** indicates everything and if you skip by **-1**, you reverse the order.

11.4   Plotting

Pandas implicitly calls **matplotlib.pyplot** for plotting purposes.

In   [17]: data['NASDAQCOM'].plot( )

If you use plt library directly, you need to add a few more lines of code to add labels and modify the graph. Pandas incorporates some of the graphic functions in the arguments of .plot( ). Try add the following examples in the function arguments.:

title = 'Nasdaq Composite Index'
style = 'r.'
xlim = [0,10000]
grid = True

Line style uses the same matplotlib arguments we learned in Chapter 9.

There are other types of graphs, such as bar charts or pie charts, that you can plot from Pandas. We will discuss these in later chapters.

11.5   DataFrame from Scratch

Pandas lets you create a DataFrame object from scratch with the **pd.DataFrame( )** function. Let's make a DataFrame that stores yearly closing prices of NASDAQ® and NYSE®.

```
06 import pandas as pd
07 year = ["1998", "1999", "2000", "2001", "2002"]
08 Nasdaq = [2192.69, 4069.31, 2470.52, 1950.40, 1335.51]
09 NYSE = [6299.93, 6876.10, 6945.57, 6236.39, 5000.00]
10
11 stock = pd.DataFrame(Nasdaq, index=year, columns=['Nasdaq'])
12 stock['NYSE'] = NYSE
13
14 stock['NYSE'].plot( )
15 stock['Nasdaq'].plot( )
```

Line 11 shows that the three basic ingredients of a DataFrame object, or any spreadsheet data. There are data in columns, index, and headers. The syntax for pd.DataFrame( ) arguments is pretty self-explanatory. Here I start with one column DataFrame and add one more with line 16. A column of data can be in the form of a list or a data array.

There are many other ways to create DataFrame objects, such as using dictionaries. I will introduce some of them in later chapters.

11.6 Export a csv File

Once you are done with your work on the DataFrame object, you can export it as a csv file that can be used in other applications, such as Excel.

In [18]: data.to_csv("test.csv")

The function **.to_csv( )** takes one argument, i.e. the file name with .csv extension you intend. You don't see any output in IPython console, but the file is created in the directory.

11.7 Exercises

Questions with asterisks have sample solutions on the book's website (www.csandaa.com/python-book).

1.* Write a Python program to import NASDAQCOM.csv as a DataFrame object. Then create 26 columns. Each column has a header from the 26 alphabets and the cells in each column should store just the header alphabet.

2. Import NASDAQCOM.csv as a DataFrame object. Clean up the missing data. Then write a Python program to do the following.

   (a) Create a column to store calculated daily returns of the Nasdaq Composite.

   (b) Find the dates when Nasdaq have more than 5% in daily returns.

   (c) Export the DataFrame in 2(b).

3. Write a Python program to find the peak value of the Nasdaq Composite during the dot com bubble.

4.* Grade sheet. Create a DataFrame object that stores five students' grades. Specifically, your DataFrame should look like the following.

ID	Gender	Grade
1	M	C+
2	M	B
3	F	A-
4	M	A
5	F	B-

Chapter 12

Pandas: Financial Data

Both professional and amateur finance researchers use Python to test their ideas. By "test ideas", I mean they implement trading strategies using historical data to see if the methods work. Proprietary data allows better accuracy and availability, but the internet also has many free sources to offer. To exemplify using Python in finance, free online resources are more than enough. In this chapter, I will show you what financial data obtained from the internet looks like.

12.1   Historical Stock Prices from Yahoo! Finance®

The use of free online financial data is restricted in their distribution. So instead of having data examples available on the book's website, I will show you how to get the data from online resources. The examples I have use data obtained in the same way. Specifically, we will use data from Yahoo! Finance®.

More sophisticated researchers have the tendency to automatize the process of getting data online. There are indeed various free libraries of functions that allow you to access sites like Yahoo! Finance®. But we should remember that these sites can change their access policy without having the need to consult or inform users. After all, they pay for the data and we don't. Indeed, both Yahoo! Finance® and Google Finance®, another popular site, have stopped API access by robots. It is a bit tedious if you want to test your ideas with many stocks, but for illustration purpose, manually downloaded data are more than enough.

Go to Yahoo! Finance's website (finance.yahoo.com) to download the historical prices of Tesla, Inc. I will use the automaker's shares as an example in this chapter. Here are the steps:

1. Type in the ticker TSLA in the search bar of the main Yahoo! Finance® page.

2. On the main TSLA stock page, click on the tab **Historical Data**.

3. Change **Time Period** and **Frequency** to the desired time frame. Make sure you hit the button **Apply** before your next move. I will use the five year period between 6/1/2010 and 5/31/2015 (the first five years after Tesla went public) with monthly frequency.

4. Click on **Download Data**. The data file is in csv format and stored in your download directory. Move it to your Python working directory and you are good to go.

12.2   Stock Prices as a DataFrame Object

The spreadsheet can now be turned into a DataFrame object.

```
01 import pandas as pd
02 data = pd.read_csv('TSLA.csv', parse_dates = True, index_col = 0)
```

In the arguments of read_csv( ) function, I introduce a new input **parse_dates = True**. Pandas can recognize various date format if you ask it to parse the data. This is very useful in financial data analysis as most of them are time series data.

Let's take a look at the data by typing in IPython console the following.

```
In   [1]: data.head( )
Out [1]:
```

	Open	High	Low	Close	Adj Close	Volume
DATE						
2010-06-01	19.000000	30.420000	17.540001	23.830000	23.830000	35953400
2010-07-01	25.000000	25.920000	14.980000	19.940001	19.940001	64575800
2010-08-01	20.500000	22.180000	17.389999	19.480000	19.480000	15038200
2010-09-01	19.620001	23.160000	19.500000	20.410000	20.410000	18045900
2010-10-01	20.690001	21.870001	20.000000	21.840000	21.840000	6547800

It looks just like the Excel spreadsheet. We can also plot the stock price series.

```
In   [2]: data['Adj Close'].plot( )
```

Since Tesla is not a dividend-paying stock, its closing prices are the same as adjusted closing prices.

You can use the script we learn in the last chapter to create a column in your DataFrame to store TSLA's return series. Or you can use the built-in Pandas function **.pct_change( )**.

In   [2]: data['Return']=data['Adj Close'].pct_change( )

In   [3]: data.head( )
Out [3]:

	Open	High	Low	Close	Adj Close	Volume
DATE						
2010-06-01	19.000000	30.420000	17.540001	23.830000	23.830000	35953400
2010-07-01	25.000000	25.920000	14.980000	19.940001	19.940001	64575800
2010-08-01	20.500000	22.180000	17.389999	19.480000	19.480000	15038200
2010-09-01	19.620001	23.160000	19.500000	20.410000	20.410000	18045900
2010-10-01	20.690001	21.870001	20.000000	21.840000	21.840000	6547800

	Open
DATE	
2010-06-01	NaN
2010-07-01	-0.163240
2010-08-01	-0.023069
2010-09-01	0.047741
2010-10-01	0.0700641

When applying **.pct_change( )**, you need to make sure the dates are in ascending order. When we move from prices to returns, we lose one data point. **NaN**, as in the first row of the data, can make further calculation problematic. We can drop the row by

In   [4]: data = data.dropna( )

12.3   More Indexing

As we learned in the last chapter, a DataFrame object can be selected and sliced by **.iloc( )** and **.loc( )** methods. The former is on the positions of the cells and the latter on the date index. Since we have parsed dates into date objects, Pandas allows flexible date format expressions. For example, the following two lines have the same outcome.

In   [5]: data.loc["6/1/2011"]

In   [6]: data.loc["2011-6-1"]
Out [6]:

```
Open         3.000000e+01
High         3.150000e+01
Low          2.550000e+01
Close        2.913000e+01
Adj Close    2.913000e+01
Volume       3.972730e+07
Return      -3.351029e-02
Name: 2011-06-01 00:00:00, dtype: float64
```

We can also find the date of any specific value by using the **.index** method.

In   [7]: data.index[data['Adj Close'] == data.iloc[5,4]]
Out [7]: DatetimeIndex(['2010-12-01'], dtype='datetime64[ns]', name='Date', freq=None)

12.4   Summary Statistics

When we get our hands on a dataset, we always visualize it first by plotting the series. We also want to look at its summary statistics. For example,

In   [8]: data['Return'].describe( )
Out [8]:
```
count    59.000000
mean      0.055015
std       0.186678
min      -0.246250
25%      -0.071550
50%       0.011667
75%       0.146748
max       0.810706
Name: Return, dtype: float64
```

As it shows in the output, Tesla, as a stock, has a positive average monthly return. It can go up to 81% return in a month or as low as -25%.

Many of the numbers in the summary statistics table can be extracted directly. For instance,

In   [9]: data['Return'].std( )
Out [9]: 0.18667759663546366

In [10]: data['Return'].median( )
Out [10]: 0.011667385333066438

To figure out the value of a specific percentile, you can use **.quantile( )**. The following line gives you 95% cutoff of the value distribution.

In [11]: data['Return'].quantile(.95)
Out [11]: 0.35702752849581254

12.5 Time Series

Most financial data are time series. That's the reason why we emphasize on parsing dates and setting dates as the index. When we operate on time series data, we often have to resample them into different frequencies, such as from daily to monthly. Pandas has built-in methods to deal with these resampling exercises.

To illustrate the point of resampling, I will download the *daily* Tesla prices from Yahoo! Finance® for the same period. I changed the csv file name to TSLA_d.csv.

```
01 import pandas as pd
02 data = pd.read_csv('TSLA_d.csv', parse_dates = True, index_col = 0)
03 data = data.resample('M').first( )
```

In [12]: data.head( )
Out [12]:

	Open	High	Low	Close	Adj Close	Volume
DATE						
2010-06-30	19.000000	25.000000	17.540001	23.889999	23.889999	18766300
2010-07-31	25.000000	25.920000	20.270000	21.959999	21.959999	8218800
2010-08-31	20.500000	20.969999	20.330000	20.920000	20.920000	7181000
2010-09-30	19.620001	20.450001	19.600000	20.450001	20.410000	494900
2010-10-31	20.690001	20.750000	20.309999	20.600000	20.600000	597700

The parameter in **.resample( )** is for the desired data frequency. Here is a list for such frequencies:

"A": annual
"Q": quarterly
"M": monthly
"W": weekly
"D": daily
"H": hourly
"T": by the minute
"S": by the second

The secondary method **.last( )** is to tell Pandas to use the last trading date of the month as the monthly price. If **.first( )** is used, the first data point of the month will be used. But this sampling difference is what causes the confusion. If you look at the monthly data from Yahoo! Finance®, shown in the beginning of this chapter, and the one we just resampled from daily data. There are obvious differences. The reason is that Yahoo! Finance ® converts daily to monthly by picking the last trading date of the month, but shows as the first day of the month. So the date labels are not correct in Yahoo! Finance®.

But if we resample it on our own from daily data, it will only be correct if we use .last( ). If we re-sample with .first( ), Pandas will collect data of the first trading date of the month, but in the index column, it will show end-of-the-month date. That's a quirkiness involved in resampling. The only way not to get confused is to look at original daily data.

You can also use **.mean( )** to take a simple average of daily prices, but this is generally discouraged in a time series analysis for the potential serial correlation problem.

12.6   Exercises

Questions with asterisks have sample solutions on the book's website (www.csandaa.com/python-book).

1.* Stock trading is considered by some as a random event like a coin toss. We can write a Python program to quickly evaluate such a sentiment. Download from Yahoo! Finance® the entire daily price series of SPY. We learned about SPY in Exercise 5 of Chapter 7. We will use the popular SPY ETF for this exercise.

   (a) Create a new column in your SPY data file called **CO**. If a trading day has a higher Adj Close price than Open, record **1** in the new column, **0** otherwise. Report the percentage of SPY's trading days that have higher close than open prices.

   (b) Create another new column in your SPY data file called **Up**. If a trading day has a higher Adj Close price than the previous day's, record **1** in the new column, **0** otherwise. Report the percentage of SPY's trading days that have a price increase from the previous day.

   (c) How do we know exercises in (a) and (b) are really different from a coin toss?

2. Download from Yahoo! Finance® the daily price records for SPY and BND. BND is also an exchange-traded fund. It is officially known as **Vanguard® Total Bond Market ETF**. The ETF is exclusively invested in fixed income securities.

   (a) Write a Python program to compare SPY and BND's summary statistics. Comment on the results.

   (b) Redo part (a), but this time, restrict your data period from 3/1/2009 to 12/31/2016.

3. Write a Python program to report the date in your data when SPY has the largest-ever daily return.

4.* Write a Python program to resample SPY daily price series to monthly and weekly frequencies, using the **.mean( )** method. Plot the two new time series on the same chart. Do you observe a trading signal?

Chapter 13

Financial Application: Technical Analysis

Traders who rely on technical analysis, such as chart reading, are called chartists. They uncover profitable trading patterns from historical data and implement the strategies in the market. The job is perfect for Python. But it is a vast field and we can only scratch the surface.

As a believer in market efficiency, I doubt that publicly known technical trading rules can deliver abnormal profits. People who try to sell technical trading signals are the pickaxes peddlers during a gold rush. It is then a natural question to ask why we bother learning technical trading rules if they don't appear to work. The answer is simple. We can't rule out proprietary rules' efficacy. By definition, proprietary rules are only known to the proprietors. If the rules work, there is no incentives for the traders to publicize them. If they don't, there is no incentive for the traders to keep going. By the sheer number of successful technical traders, I cannot rule out the possibility of working technical rules. Therefore, learning how to implement technical trading rules is not necessarily meaningless.

Unfortunately, what I can demonstrate here are only public and mostly useless technical trading rules.

The code I will be showing is to do the so-called **backtesting**. In backtesting, we put ourselves at a point of time in the past and are unaware of what is to come. We implement the trading rule at that particular point of time. Then we look at the performance of the strategy and infer from the result.

13.1   Filter Rules

A filter rule is to act on filtered results of a stock price movement. Once a stock passes the filter rule, the trader either buys or sells on the spot. For example, a momentum filter rule can ask a trader to buy a stock when it is 3% or more higher than a previous low and to sell it when is 3% or more below its previous high.

Let's use TSLA daily prices to demonstrate such a rule and test its validity. In the following example, I imagine on any given trading day, the trader looks at his position and makes a decision. If the trader has the stock, he looks for a selling signal. If he doesn't, he looks for the buying signal.

The signal is determined by the trading day's open price and the local high or low price. Say, the trader is in position. If he sees the opening price is 3% or more lower than the previous peak, he sells. The following code captures these actions by creating a new column called **Position**.

```
01 import pandas as pd
02 data = pd.read_csv('TSLA_d.csv', parse_dates = True, index_col=0)
03
04 data['Position'] = 0 #1 is in, 0 is out.
05 rule = .03 #Establish the filter threshold.
06 low = data.iloc[0, 3] #Initiate local low.
07 high = data.iloc[0, 3] #Initiate local high.
08
09 for i in range(1, len(data)):
10     if data.iloc[i-1, 6] == 1: #In position, look for sell signal.
11         if data.iloc[i, 0]/high < (1-rule): #Signal to sell at open.
12             data.iloc[i:, 6] = 0
13             low = data.iloc[i, 3] #Reset local low after selling.
14
15     else: #Out of postion, look for buy signal.
16         if data.iloc[i, 0]/low > (1+rule): #Signal to buy at open.
17             data.iloc[i:, 6] = 0
18             high = data.iloc[i, 3]#Reset local high after buying.
19
20     if data.iloc[i, 3] < low: #Update low.
21         low = data.iloc[i, 3]
22     elif data.iloc[i, 3] > high: #Update high.
23         high = data.iloc[i, 3]
```

At this point, we "went back to history" to establish our in or out position in Tesla. Now I will show you how to look at the performance and compare it to a simple buy-and-hold strategy.

In essence, we try to see how "wealth" is built up using the rule. Wealth grows at the rate of Tesla's price change if the trader holds a position. It stays the same if the trader doesn't hold a position. During the days when the trader moves from in to out position, the wealth is calculated based on the number of shares he owns on the previous day. Then we multiply the number with the opening price of the day. Wealth is calculated in a similar way when moving from out to in position.

```
24 data['Wealth'] = 100 #Using $100 to invest with the filter rule.
25 for i in range(1, len(data)):
26     if data.iloc[i-1, 6] == 0 and data.iloc[i, 6] == 0: #Out pos to out pos.
27         data.iloc[i, 7] = data.iloc[i-1, 7]
28     elif data.iloc[i-1, 6] == 0 and data.iloc[i, 6] == 1: #Out to in pos.
```

```
29          data.iloc[i, 7] = data.iloc[i-1, 7]/data.iloc[i, 0]*data.iloc[i, 3]
30      elif data.iloc[i-1, 6] == 1 and data.iloc[i, 6] == 1: #In to in pos.
31          data.iloc[i, 7] = data.iloc[i-1, 7]/data.iloc[i-1,3]*data.iloc[i, 3]
32      else: #In to out pos.
33          data.iloc[i, 7] = data.iloc[i-1, 7]/data.iloc[i-1, 3]*data.iloc[i,0]
```

The **Wealth** column I just created let us know how much money the initial $100 grows into, but the absolute value of the ending balance means little, if we don't have a benchmark. The following code shows how to standardize the benchmark buy-and-hold strategy. You can imagine a passive investor who puts in $100 in Tesla stock at the beginning. The result will be the ending balance of such a stragegy.

```
34 data['New Price'] = 100
35 for i in range(1, len(data)):
36      data.iloc[i, 8]=data.iloc[i-1, 8]/data.iloc[i-1, 4]*data.iloc[i,4]
```

We can plot the two wealth series to compare their performance.

```
37 data["New Price"].plot(style = "b.") #A blue dotted line for the buy-and-hold.
38 data["Wealth"].plot(style = "r") #A red line for the filter rule.
```

The graphic comparison is not the most scientific way to measure the performance of any trading strategy. For that, we need to know the benchmark return series. But a picture is worth a thousand words. By looking at the following graph, we are safe to say there is no free money in this case. We haven't even talked about transaction costs!

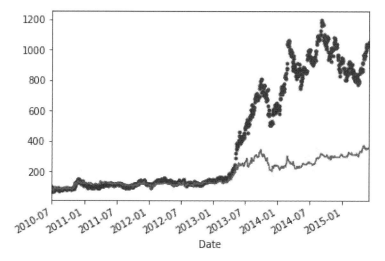

You can try to change the filter threshold and time period to see if you can "data mine" a satisfying rule. To change the filter threshold, you just modify line 5. To change the time period, you can insert the following in line 3:

```
03 data = data.loc["1/1/2013": "6/30/2013"]
```

13.2   Simple Moving Average

Trend-following speculators often look at moving averages of stock prices. A moving average is an arithmetic average of several consecutive trading days' closing prices. For example, the 50-day moving average is to look back 50 trading days first. The chart-maker then adds up all the 50 closing prices and divides the sum by 50.

We can construct various moving average series by looking back various amounts of days. The popular ones are 20, 50, 100, and 250. Because moving averages smooth out short-term volatility, traders can spot stock trends easier by looking at moving averages. Trading signals emerge from the crossovers of varying moving averages. A typical Simple Moving Average (SMA) trading rule is to buy when a short-term moving average crosses a long-term one from below. The crossover indicates an upward trend. It becomes a sell signal when the short-term crosses the long-term from above.

Let's use our Tesla daily prices to create moving averages and see if we can detect trading signals.

```
01 import pandas as pd
02 import numpy as np
03 import matplotlib.pyplot as plt
04 data = pd.read_csv('TSLA_d.csv', parse_dates = True, index_col=0)
05
06 data['Adj Close'].plot(style = 'k')#Look at the price chart first.
07
07 def ma(original, period): #Define a function to calculate moving averages.
08      """
09      Take in original prices as a list.
10      Return a moving average series as a list.
11      Period is a number for the lookback period.
12      """
13      ma = [ ]
14      n = len(original)
15      for i in range(period):
16          ma.append(float('nan')) #No moving averages in the beginning.
17      for i in range(period, n):
18          ma.append(np.mean(original[i-period : i]))
19      return ma
20
21 data['20'] = ma(list(data['Adj Close']), 20)
22 data['50'] = ma(list(data['Adj Close']), 50)
23 data['250'] = ma(list(data['Adj Close']), 250)
24
25 plt.figure( )
26 data['20'].plot(style = 'b,')
27 data['250'].plot(style = 'r')
```

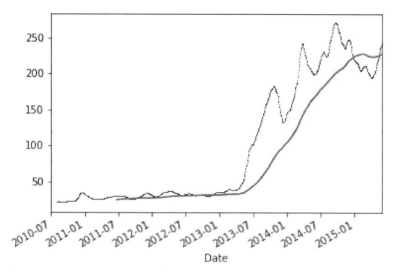

As you can see in the graphic output above, the short-term, blue, dotted 20-day moving average crosses the long-term, red 250-day moving average from below in 2012. Following that trading signal, Tesla went on a spectacular run.

13.3 Exercises

Questions with asterisks have sample solutions on the book's website (www.csandaa.com/python-book).

1. Long and Short. In the example in the text, we only have long positions and stay on the sideline when the signal is to sell. Modify the code to accommodate the strategy that uses both long and short signals.

2.* Momentum vs. Contrarian. A momentum strategy is to buy a stock when it is hot and sell when not. A contrarian one is to do the contrary. A contrarian investor sells a stock when it is hot and buys when not. The strategy in the Filter Rules section is a momentum one. How do you change it to a contrarian strategy?

3. Fade the Gap. If a stock opens a day's trading with an abruptly higher or lower price than the previous day's close price, it is said to "gap up" or "gap down." A trading strategy is to fill the gap by shorting the stock when it gaps up or buying when gaps down. Then the trader exits the position at the close of the trading day. No overnight positions. Let's test this strategy with real stock data.

   (a) Go to Yahoo! Finance to download the historical prices for a stock that interests you.

   (b) Let's work on a gap-down strategy. If we define a gap as 3% or more departure from the previous day's close price, shrink your data to contain only those dates.

   (c) Find the percentage of gap-down days that see a higher close price than open.

(d) Calculate the daily rate of return of the data in in (b).

(e) Report the average rate of return of "Fill the Gap" strategy.

Chapter 14

Pandas: Data and Dictionaries

Before analyzing data, we often need to clean up the raw data and make changes for the data to be usable. Pandas is a convenient tool for such tasks.

In this chapter, I will also introduce the **dictionary** object. It is a versatile tool that coders can't live without.

14.1 Dynamic Code Generation with exec( )

If you download data from sources such as Yahoo! Finance® for a large project, say 100 stocks, you will soon be overwhelmed by the manual work. Even when you use APIs to access the source, you will still have to face the tedious task of importing the data files one at a time. Here I am going to show you how the **exec( )** function can help you avoid copying and pasting 100 times for the same task.

exec( ) generates code dynamically by evaluating a string at a time. If you can find a way to replace part of the string to be evaluated, you can automatize the repetitive work. For example, in part of the string, you can insert a stock symbol. You then run a for loop to replace the symbol with items from a stock symbol list. Here is the code.

```
01 import pandas as pd
02 import matplotlib.pyplot as plt
03 stock=["GS", "NKE", "DIS", "XOM", "PFE", "MSFT"]
04 #Make sure you first download prices for these 6 stocks to your working directory.
05 for i in stock:
06     exec(i+ '=pd.read_csv("'+ i +'.csv", parse_dates=True, index_col=0)')
07     exec(i+ ' ='+ i +'.resample("M").last( )')
08     exec(i+ '["Return"]='+ i +'["Adj Close"].pct_change( )')
```

In the for loop's first iteration, **i** is **"GS"**. So line 6 is treated as

GS = pd.read_csv("GS.csv", parse_dates=True, index_col=0)

Here I concatenate the strings with simple addition operation. You also see the reason why Python needs two sets of quotation marks. It is sometimes confusing to write the proper argument for the exec( ) function, but you can always start your command line without exec( ) as the above line shows and make modification from there.

This example only processes 6 stocks, but you can easily extend the stock list to include 100 or even more!

14.2   Merging Data

The stock prices we just imported and turned into return series can be combined into one big DataFrame by using the **.join( )** method.

09 data = GS.join(GS, how="inner", rsuffix="_GS")
10 data = data.join(NKE, how="inner", rsuffix="_NKE")
11 data = data.join(DIS, how="inner", rsuffix="_DIS")
12 data = data.join(XOM, how="inner", rsuffix="_XOM")
13 data = data.join(PFE, how="inner", rsuffix="_PFE")
14 data = data.join(MSFT, how="inner", rsuffix="_MSFT")

When we merge data with .join( ), we can picture that we put two DataFrames side by side. Specifically, we use **left.join(right)** to understand how the method is used. A DataFrame on the left is joined to one on the right and they share the same index. Since the left and right might have different lengths in data, we need to pick the union or the intersection of the two: **how="inner"** for the intersection and **how="outer"** for a union.

When two DataFrames with the same column header names are joined or merged, we should put suffixes to the headers to distinguish them. But because suffixes will only be attached when they show up in double, I create a redundant copy to retain GS's header in line 09. Line 09 to 14 can also be taken care of with a for loop and an exec( ) function.

15 data = GS
16 for i in stock:
17   exec('data = data.join(' + i +', how = "inner", rsuffix = "_' + i + '")')

Frequently, we have financial data from different time periods. If we want to merge them "vertically", meaning stacking them along the time index, we use the **pd.concat( )** function. In the argument, we supply a list of DataFrames that are to be concatenated. See Exercise 2 of this Chapter for an example.

We can take a look at the stocks we just put together.

18 data=data.loc["1/1/2009" : "12/31/2016"] #Select a desired time period.
19 data=data.dropna( ) #Drop non-available values.

```
20 describe = [ ] #Initiate a list to store summary statistics.
21 for i in stock:
22      exec('describe.append(data["Return_' + i +'"].describe( ))')
23 summary = pd.DataFrame(describe)
```

In lines 20-22, I use the exec( ) function to create a list that keeps the summary statistics (recall the **.describe( )** we learned in Chapter 12). The function **pd.DataFrame( )** can stack up the summary statistics to form a DataFrame object. Take a look in IPython console.

In   [1]: summary
Out [1]:

	count	mean	std	min	25%	50%
Return_GS	96.0	0.015566	0.085291	-0.186457	-0.047975	0.016521
Return_NKE	96.0	0.017828	0.064944	-0.188575	-0.027653	0.013858
Return_DIS	96.0	0.019276	0.065768	-0.189071	-0.012521	0.019304
Return_XOM	96.0	0.004640	0.045950	-0.107712	-0.019903	0.002802
Return_PFE	96.0	0.011079	0.054550	-0.176736	-0.024546	0.008928
Return_MSFT	96.0	0.016623	0.067813	-0.151394	-0.030800	0.020493

	75%	max
Return_GS	0.072249	0.234121
Return_NKE	0.063301	0.173584
Return_DIS	0.059709	0.205947
Return_XOM	0.041936	0.112844
Return_PFE	0.051936	0.149860
Return_MSFT	0.056729	0.196261

A useful tool for DataFrame objects is **.transpose( )**. You can turn rows into columns and vice versa.

In   [2]: summary.transpose( )
Out [2]:

	Ret_GS	Ret_NKE	Ret_DIS	Ret_XOM	Ret_PFE	Ret_MSFT
count	96.000000	96.000000	96.000000	96.000000	96.000000	96.000000
mean	0.015566	0.017828	0.019276	0.004640	0.011079	0.016623
std	0.085291	0.064944	0.065768	0.045950	0.054550	0.067813
min	-0.186457	-0.188575	-0.189071	-0.107712	-0.176736	-0.151394
25%	-0.047975	-0.027653	-0.012521	-0.019903	-0.024546	-0.030800
50%	0.016521	0.013858	0.019304	0.002802	0.008928	0.020493
75%	0.072249	0.063301	0.059709	0.041936	0.051936	0.056729
max	0.234121	0.173584	0.205947	0.112844	0.149860	0.196261

14.3   Bar Charts as a Tool to Visualize Data

Let's take at look at the returns and standard deviations of these monthly returns in two charts.

```
24 plt.figure( ) #To start a graph
25 summary['mean'].plot(kind='barh', color='b', title='Average Return')
```

26 **plt.figure( )** #To start a new graph
27 **summary['std'].plot(kind='barh', color='r', title='Standard Deviation')**

Here Pandas implicitly calls the .plot( ) method from the **matplotlib.pyplot**, which we imported in line 2. You will see a couple of horizontal bar charts. This is what it means by 'barh' in the **kind = "barh"** argument. If vertical bars are desired, change the argument to **kind="bar"**. From the two bar charts shown below, can you see the high risk—high return relationship?

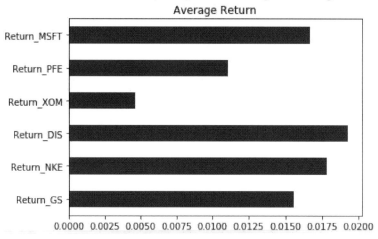

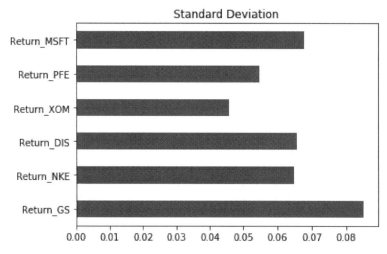

14.4 Dictionaries

There is another way to handle the bar chart without the help of Pandas. Let's also use this opportunity to learn a new object type in Python–**dictionary**.

The dictionary object (also known as dict) allows mixed types, just like lists. It has two parts: **keys** and **values**. With keys, we can quickly look up corresponding values. Specifically, a dictionary has this structure:

{key1: value1, key2: value2,......}

Lists use square brackets, while dictionaries have curly braces. Unlike lists, dictionaries are not ordered sequentially. The order appearing in the output is not fixed. So you don't index dictionaries by positions, but by keys.

We can generate a dictionary with a few different methods. But let's look at some dict basics.

In [3]: example ={"a": 1,"b": 2, "c": 3}
In [4]: example
Out [4]: {'a': 1, 'b': 2, 'c': 3}

In [5]: example['a']
Out [5]: 1

From line command 5 we see that square brackets are a universal way to index sequences in Python, regardless of the object types.

```
In   [6]: example.keys( )
Out [6]: dict_keys(['a', 'b', 'c'])
In   [7]: list(example.keys( ))
Out [7]: ['a', 'b', 'c']
```

Line command 7 is a short-cut to extract dict keys. We can do the same thing to dict values.

```
In   [8]: example.values( )
Out [8]: dict_values([1, 2, 3])
In   [9]: list(example.values( ))
Out [9]: [1, 2, 3]
```

We can also "zip" any two lists into a dict.

```
In   [10]: x = list(example.keys( ))
In   [11]: y = list(example.values( ))
In   [12]: new_example=dict(zip(x, y))
In   [13]: new_example
Out [13]: {'a': 1, 'b': 2, 'c': 3}
```

Both command lines 3 and 12 create a dictionary object. These object generating methods are called **literals**. After a dict is created, we can append a new item by

```
In   [14]: example["d"] = 4
In   [15]: example
Out [15]: {'a': 1, 'b': 2, 'c': 3, 'd': 4}
```

Or we can delete an item by

```
In   [16]: del example["d"]
In   [17]: example
Out [17]: {'a': 1, 'b': 2, 'c': 3}
```

Or

```
In   [18]: example.pop('c')
Out [18]: 3
In   [19]: example
Out [19]: {'a': 1, 'b': 2}
```

Now let's revisit our stock example. This time we will employ the dict objects.

```
28 x = [ ] #Create two lists to store returns and standard deviations.
```

```
29 y = [ ]
30
31 for i in stock:
32      exec('x.append(data["Return_'+ i +' "].mean( ))')
33       exec('y.append(data["Return_'+ i +' "].std( ))')
34
35 ret = dict(zip(stock, x))
36 sigma = dict(zip(stock, y))
37
38 plt.figure( )
39 plt.bar(range(len(ret)), ret.values( ), color='b')
40 #You can change to barh( ) for horizontal bar chart.
41 plt.xticks(range(len(ret)), list(ret.keys( )))
42 #Change to yticks( ) for horizontal bar chart.
43 plt.title('Average Return')
44
45 plt.figure( )
46 plt.bar(range(len(sigma)), sigma.values( ), color='r')
47 #Change to barh( ) for horizontal bar chart.
48 plt.xticks(range(len(sigma)), list(sigma.keys( )))
49 #Change to yticks( ) for horizontal
50 plt.title('Standard Deviation')
```

In a scatter plot, we use plt.plot(x, y). For a bar chart, the syntax is similar–plt.bar(x, y), where **x** is usually values representing categories. So in lines 39 and 41, I use a trick to first create a range object to store x's and then replace these x's with the category names. The output graphs should look the same as the ones in the previous section.

14.5 Exercises

Questions with asterisks have sample solutions on the book's website (www.csandaa.com/python-book).

1.* Go online to find the two digit state code (e.g., Iowa is 16) and save it in a .csv file. Also find the postal code for states (e.g., Iowa is IA.) and save it in another .csv file. Use the two files to create a dictionary object that has all 50 state postal codes as the keys and the numeric codes as the values. Make sure the two files have the same alphabetical order for the state names.

2.* Concatenate data. **pd.join( ) or pd.merge( )** extend the columns for each observation. If we, however, want to add observations to the columns, i.e., stacking up data, we need to use **pd.concat(o)**, where **o** is a list of data objects to be stacked. Your assignment is to concatenate 5 neighboring states' census data and plot a bar chart for the 10 largest counties (by population) in these five states.

   (a) Read in the five datasets (ia.csv, il.csv, mn.csn, mo.csv, and wi.csv) with Pandas from the course website. When you read csv, make sure the **index_col = None** is included.

   (b) Use **pd.concat( )** to concatenate the five datasets. Make sure you add **data = data.reset_index( )** to erase each individual dataset's index and reset it for the whole.

   (c) Create a dictionary to store the 10 largest counties' names and their population (from the column **CENSUS2010POP**). To find the largest counties, you can sort the data by **data.sort_values(by = "CENSUS2010POP", ascending=False)**. Make sure in your graph output, each county also includes its state name.

3. You will use the **pandas_datareader** library to access World Bank's GDP data. Specifically, you will download the GDP data for the Group of Seven countries. G7 are Canada (CA), France (FR), Germany (DE), Italy (IT), Japan (JP), United Kingdom (GB), and United States (US).

   (a) The library and function you will use are shown in the following lines[1].

```
1 from pandas_datareader import wb
2 data = wb.download(indicator='NY.GDP.PCAP.KD', country=['US'],
start=2005, end=2015)
```

     These two lines get you US's GDP data from 2005 to 2015. Plot the time series. Note that the data is in descending order. You should change it to ascending by **data = data.sort_index(ascending=True)**.

   (b) Download G7 countries' GDP for the year 2015. Plot a bar chart.

4. The **pandas_datareader** library allows you to access Google Finance's historical prices. Go online to find the tickers for the 30 stocks in the Dow Jones Industrial Average. Use the following code to get their daily prices (Google only gives you one year's data). Then plot the thirty stocks' daily returns against daily standard deviations.

```
1 import pandas_datareader.data as web
2 stock = web.DataReader("stock", 'google')
```

---

[1]Anaconda doesn't come with the **pandas_datareader** installed. You have to go to your terminal application to install it by typing in **pip install pandas-datareader**.

Chapter 15

Pandas: Groupby

Excel has a powerful tool called **pivot tables**. Pivot tables allow you to slice a big dataset into a view that not only is more accessible to the user, but also provides insight to the convoluted original data. **Groupby** is the pivot table counterpart in Pandas.

Groupby, according to Wes McKinney (McKinney, 2012), is a three-step procedure in which the data analysts **split** the data, **apply** certain functions on the split data, and **combine** the results. Let's look at an example to see how the three steps are implemented.

15.1   A Groupby Example of the S&P 500

Go to the book's website to find a link to the website of SPDR®. The link will take you to the holding information of the SPDR® S&P 500® ETF (ticker = SPY). After downloading the spreadsheet, make sure you clean up the remarks and save it as a csv file in your Python working directory.

```
01 import pandas as pd
02 import matplotlib.pyplot as plt
03 data = pd.read_csv("spyholdings.csv", index_col=None)
```

Let's look at the data. Remember that your output is likely to be different from what I have here because the data is constantly being updated.

```
In   [1]: data.head( )
Out [1]:
```

	Name	Identifier	Weight	Sector
0	Apple Inc.	AAPL	4.091824	Information Technology
1	Microsoft Corporation	MSFT	2.927961	Information Technology
2	Amazon.com Inc.	AMZN	2.030903	Consumer Discretionary
3	Facebook Inc. Class A	FB	1.913583	Information Technology
4	Johnson & Johnson	JNJ	1.705135	Health Care

	Shares Held
0	57604170
1	85909624
2	4447816
3	26441082
4	29936184

Just as in creating a pivot table, we need to first have a target variable (sometimes referred to as a target attribute or field) in mind before we can group data. In the SPY holding data, we would like to see each sector's total weight allocation. Specifically, we'd like to see an output table like

Sector	Total Weights
Sector 1	xx%
Sector 2	yy%
:	:

With the desired output in mind, we can proceed to use the groupby tool.

04 gb_sum = data["Weight"].groupby(data["Sector"]).sum( )

The **.groupby( )** method takes in the variable to group together by and produces a special Pandas object. The object itself is not explicitly revealing any information. This is the **split** step. We split the stocks by their sectors.

Step 2 is to **apply** functions on the split data. As in line 3, we use the **.sum( )** method right after .groupby( ) because we want to add up the total weights in each sector. Now the groupby data is unpacked and we can assign it to a new variable called **gb_sum**. It is a Series object. Try in IPython console:

In   [2]: gb_sum
Out [2]:

```
Sector
Consumer Discretionary          11.771696
Consumer Staples                 7.950712
Energy                           6.017125
Financials                      14.384224
Health Care                     14.058989
Industrials                      9.986126
Information Technology          24.760454
Materials                        2.977263
Real Estate                      3.016931
Telecommunication Services       1.829148
Utilities                        3.161949
Name: Weight, dtype: float64
```

Weights by sector in the output table above reveal interesting information, but we can do better by doing the third step, **combine**. Let's organize the output.

```
05 gb_sum = gb_sum.sort_values( )
06 gb_sum.plot(kind="barh", title="S&P 500 Weights by Sector (%)"))
```

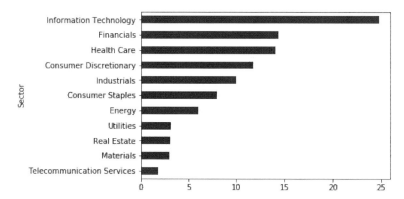

Information Technology, as a sector, has the most weight allocation in the S&P 500. This is interesting, but could the heavy weight allocation come from more IT companies in the index? We can answer the question by looking at the count of stocks in each sector and the average weight in each sector. We go back to the apply step and use two other methods: **.count( )** and **.mean( )**.

```
07 gb_count = data["Weight].groupby(data["Sector"]).count( )
08 gb_mean = data["Weight"].groupby(data["Sector"]).mean( )
09 plt.figure( )
10 sector = sector.sort_values(by="Mean", ascending=True)
11 sector["Mean"].plot(kind="barh",color="r")
```

Looking at the average weight in each sector in the following graph, we see that Information Technology is high in average weight as well, but Telecommunication Services has the highest average weight. It is not too surprising as you can see in the S&P 500 index list that there are only three big corporations in that sector: VZ (Verizon), T (AT&T), and CTL (CenturyLink).

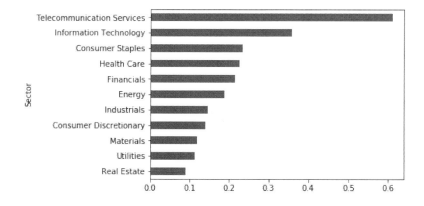

We can also collect all three data series together and create a DataFrame that can be of more use and be exported.

```
12 sector = pd.DataFrame("Weight":gb_sum,"Count":gb_count,"Mean":gb_mean)
13 sector = sector.sort_values(by="Weight", ascending=False)
14 sector.to_csv("sector.csv")
```

15.2   Groupby and Resample

Groupby can also group data by time in a similar way to the .resample( ) method we learned previously. But sometimes groupby can have outcomes that cannot be achieved by .resample( ). For example, if we suspect that the trading volume differs by the days of the weeek, we will have a hard time getting the result with .resample( ), but groupby is perfect for the job.

Let's use Tesla's daily record as an example.

```
01 import datetime as dt #Use datetime libary to determine the day of the week.
02 import pandas as pd
03 import matplotlib.pyplot as plt
04
05 data = pd.read_csv('TSLA_d.csv', parse_dates=True, index_col=0)
06 def days(date): #Define a function to convert dates to days.
07     """
08     Argument date must be a datetime object.
09     Return the day of the week.
10     """
11     start = dt.datetime(2000, 1, 1) #It's a Saturday.
12     delta = date - start
13     x = delta.days #Use .days to extract day difference of two dt objects.
14     if x % 7 == 0:
15         day = 6 #Saturday
16     elif x % 7 == 1:
17         day = 0 #Sunday
18     elif x % 7 == 2:
19         day = 1 #Monday
20     elif x % 7 == 3:
21         day = 2 #Tuesday
22     elif x % 7 == 4:
23         day = 3 #Wednesday
24     elif x % 7 == 5:
25         day = 4 #Thursday
26     else:
27         day = 5 #Friday
28     return day
29
30 data['Day'] = 0
```

```
31
32 for i in range(len(data)):
33     data.iloc[i,6] = days(data.index[i])
34
35 gb_mean = data['Volume'].groupby(data['Day']).mean( )
36
37 plt.barh(gb_mean.index, gb_mean)
38 plt.yticks(gb_mean.index, ['Monday','Tuesday','Wednesday','Thursday','Friday'])
39 plt.title('Average Trading Volume')
```

The result is shown in the following graph. Tuesday turns out to be the most traded day of the week. A caveat for interpretation of the result: we don't have distribution statistics to tell whether those days have any significant differences in trading volume.

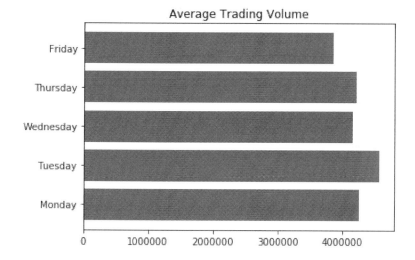

Here is the last word on Pandas for data analysis. Python with Pandas is a serious competitor to R. Groupby is only one of the tools Pandas offers for data analysis. But I will stop here and leave the rest for you to explore, as this is a book for finance, not data science.

15.3 Exercises

Questions with asterisks have sample solutions on the book's website (www.csandaa.com/python-book).

1.* Performance by sector. We will continue the example in the text, but expand the exercise by getting stock prices for each of the component stocks in the S&P 500®.

(a) Use the **pandas_datareader** library to get stock prices from Google Finance. Here are the lines of code you will need. You will have to write a for loop and use the **exec( )** to complete the task.

```
1 import pandas_datareader.data as web
2 stock = web.DataReader("stock", 'google')
```

(b) As of the time of writing this exercise, there are some quirkiness you need to fix in your spyholdings.csv before using it. Three stocks (**BRK.B**, **CCL.U**, and **BF.B**) include a **.** that won't be read by Google. Remove the **.** and the letter right after it. Secondly, **CASH_USD** is the cash portion held by the ETF. You should remove the row containing **CASH_USD** altogether. Thirdly, you need to remove three stocks that are not recognized by Google (**LMT**,**NWL**, and **NBL**). We lose the completeness in exchange for feasibility. Not too bad a trade-off. In the future, it's a good practice for you to add a counter in your for loop to see when the function stops getting data from Google.

(c) After all stocks are downloaded, create two columns in your data file (the one before you do groupby, in line 02 in the text), one called **Return** storing those stocks' returns and the other called **STD** storing standard deviations.

(d) Group your data by sector, but use **Return** and **STD** as your target values. Which sector performs the best?

2. Performance by size. We will continue the exercise in the text. The S&P 500® uses a market value weighted average to calculate the weight allocation for each stock. The weight itself is then a proxy to the stock's market cap. Create a new column in your data called **Size**. Divide the list into 4 groups with equal numbers of stocks in each and then group the data by **Size**. The target values are still the same as in Exercise 1. Do bigger companies perform better?

You can use **data["Weight"].quantile(.25)** to find the 25% cutoff, **data["Weight"].quantile(.50)** for 50%, and **data["Weight"].quantile(.75)** for 75%.

3. When a stock opens higher than the previous trading day's close, does it have higher trading volume than if it opens lower than the previous day's close? Use Tesla's daily record to answer the question.

Chapter 16

Ordinary Least Squares Regression

Ordinary Least Squares (OLS) regression is the workhorse for data analysis. Financial applications of OLS are also ubiquitous. We could have continued using pandas for regression, but it is now recommended to adopt **statsmodels.api**.

I am not presenting any theoretical derivations of OLS estimation in this book. Instead, I will go straight into how to run regression in Python. After learning how to run OLS regression, I will show a few critical applications of OLS in finance. At the end of this chapter, I will also introduce logistic regression, a useful digression from OLS.

16.1   OLS with statsmodels

Let's start our OLS regression with estimating the following model:

$income = \alpha + \beta \times test + \epsilon.$

The model is to find out whether a person's cognitive test score can explain his/her annual income. A statistically significant coefficient (β) is what we are looking for. If β turns out to be positive, we have some confidence to build the connection between a person's test score and income. The intercept α is to capture the natural income level that is not dependent on the test score and the unobserved ϵ has all other hidden factors.

Download **nlsy97.csv** from the book's website. The data includes survey result from the National Longitudinal Survey of Youth done by the Bureau of Labor Statistics. The data is cross-sectional and has only two variables: **test**, which stores the test score in percentile, and **income**, which is the self-reported annual income.

Let's look at the deta first.

```
01 import pandas as pd
02 import matplotlib.pyplot as plt
03 import statsmodels.api as sm
```

```
04 data = pd.read_csv("nlsy97.csv", index_col=None)
05 plt.plot(data["test"], data["income"], 'b.')
06 plt.xlabel("Test")
07 plt.ylabel("Income")
```

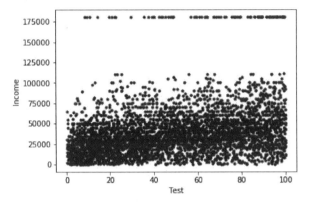

BLS truncated higher annual income to $180,331, making the scatter plot look funny. Let's delete these "outliers" to have a "cleaner" regression result.

```
08 to_delete=[ ]
09 for i in range(len(data)):
10        if data.iloc[i,1] > 180000:
11              to_delete.append(i)
12 data = data.drop(data.index[to_delete])
```

The **.drop( )** method can drop rows if given the list of index positions. Redraw the plot.

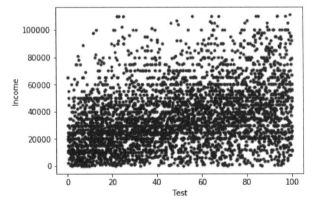

In the new graph, we can detect an upward trend line, showing a positive correlation between test scores and income levels. But to quantify such a relationship between variables, an OLS estimator is needed.

We will use the **statsmodels.api** library, but before we estimate the model, we need to specify the variables to be regressed on.

13 x = data["test"]
14 x = sm.add_constant(x)
15 y = data["income"]

Note that defult OLS in statsmodels.api doesn't include the intercept term, but almost all OLS regression models need it to force a condition required for unbiased estimation. So you should always use the function in line 14 to add the intercept. Now we can have the main action.

16 result = sm.OLS(y, x).fit( )

In the argument input for **sm.OLS( ).fit( )**, you supply your left-hand-side (y) and right-hand-side (x) variables. The method **.summary( )** gives you the summary output of the model estimates. I still remember the first time I ran regression with a package software. It was anticlimactic, as I was looking for an animated trend line appearing in the graph. Instead, I was greeted by an output table that was full of numbers. This .summary( ) is the unexciting table you are looking for in OLS regression.

17 **print(result.summary( ))**

```
                          OLS Regression Results
==============================================================================
Dep. Variable:                 income   R-squared:                       0.097
Model:                            OLS   Adj. R-squared:                  0.097
Method:                 Least Squares   F-statistic:                     449.5
Date:                Thu, 08 Mar 2018   Prob (F-statistic):           7.47e-95
Time:                        10:22:35   Log-Likelihood:                -47745.
No. Observations:                4191   AIC:                         9.549e+04
Df Residuals:                    4189   BIC:                         9.551e+04
Df Model:                           1
Covariance Type:            nonrobust
==============================================================================
                 coef    std err          t      P>|t|      [95.0% Conf. Int.]
------------------------------------------------------------------------------
const         2.411e+04    652.192     36.971      0.000     2.28e+04  2.54e+04
test           244.3418     11.524     21.202      0.000      221.748   266.936
==============================================================================
Omnibus:                      290.117   Durbin-Watson:                   1.952
Prob(Omnibus):                  0.000   Jarque-Bera (JB):              352.370
Skew:                           0.682   Prob(JB):                     3.05e-77
Kurtosis:                       3.395   Cond. No.                         111.
==============================================================================
```

Can you confirm the prior that people with higher test scores make more money? But you should be careful with the interpretation, as we know the omitted variable bias is present in this model.

Frequently, you need to extract estimated model parameters from the result. You can use the following methods:

result.params : coefficients
result.tvalues : t-values
result.pvalues : p-values
result.rsquared : R^2 .

For example, to extract the intercept value, you can type in IPython console:

In   [1]: result.params[0]
Out [1]: 24111.98505688793

16.2   CAPM Regression

The Capital Asset Pricing Model (Sharpe, 1964) is a breakthrough development in the history of finance. The CAPM is probably the most famous acronym in finance. In a nutshell, the CAPM describes a financial asset's systematic risk (β) by

$\bar{R} - R_f = \alpha + \beta(\bar{R}_m - R_f) + \epsilon$, where

$\bar{R}$ is the individual asset's expected return, R_f risk-free's return, and $\bar{R}_m$ the market portfolio's expected return.

If we regress an asset's realized excess return on the market risk premium, assuming ϵ is a white noise, the estimated coefficient of the explanatory variable is β.

Let's use Tesla's daily record to illustrate how β is estimated. For the risk-free and market portfolio's expected returns, we will use the gold standard in finance research, i.e. Prof. Ken French's Data Library at
http://mba.tuck.dartmouth.edu/pages/faculty/ken.french/data_library.html

Find the csv file for **Fama/French 3 Factors [Daily]** and save it to your working directory. When you have your hands on French's csv files, make sure you clean up remarks and footers. You should only have date and data columns with appropriate column headers. Also note that these factor premiums are already in percentages. A number 1 means 1% or 0.01.

```
01 import pandas as pd
02 import matplotlib.pyplot as plt
03 import statsmodels.api as sm
04 french = pd.read_csv("french.csv", parse_dates=True, index_col=0)
05 tsla = pd.read_csv("TSLA_d.csv", parse_dates=True, index_col=0)
```

Let's look at the data first.

In [2]: french.head( )
Out [2]:

	Mkt-RF	SMB	HML	RF
1926-07-01	0.10	-0.24	-0.28	0.009
1926-07-02	0.45	-0.32	-0.08	0.009
1926-07-06	0.17	0.27	-0.35	0.009
1926-07-07	0.09	-0.59	0.03	0.009
1926-07-08	0.21	-0.36	0.15	0.009

In [3]: tsla.head( )
Out [3]:

Date	Open	High	Low	Close	Adj Close	Volume
2010-06-29	19.000000	25.00	17.540001	23.889999	23.889999	18766300
2010-06-30	25.790001	30.42	23.299999	23.830000	23.830000	17187100
2010-07-01	25.000000	25.92	20.270000	21.959999	21.959999	8218800
2010-07-02	23.000000	23.10	18.709999	19.200001	19.200001	5139800
2010-07-06	20.000000	20.00	15.830000	16.110001	16.110001	6866900

The two data sets vary in length. We have to sacrifice some data to synchronize the two sets. We also need to convert Tesla's prices into returns before we can run OLS regression.

```
06 tsla["Return"] = tsla["Adj Close"].pct_change( )
07 data = french.join(tsla, how="inner")
08 data = data.dropna( )
```

Now we can finally run OLS.

```
09 y = data["Return"]*100 - data["RF"] #French's data are already in percentages.
10 x = data["Mkt-RF"]
11 x = sm.add_constant(x)
12 CAPM = sm.OLS(y, x).fit( )
13 print(CAPM.summary( ))
```

```
                           OLS Regression Results
===============================================================================
Dep. Variable:                      y   R-squared:                      0.133
Model:                            OLS   Adj. R-squared:                 0.132
Method:                 Least Squares   F-statistic:                    189.1
Date:                Thu, 08 Mar 2018   Prob (F-statistic):          3.89e-40
Time:                        14:03:21   Log-Likelihood:               -3232.4
No. Observations:                1237   AIC:                            6469.
Df Residuals:                    1235   BIC:                            6479.
Df Model:                           1
Covariance Type:            nonrobust
===============================================================================
                 coef    std err          t      P>|t|      [95.0% Conf. Int.]
-------------------------------------------------------------------------------
const          0.1603      0.094      1.702      0.089      -0.024      0.345
Mkt-RF         1.3029      0.095     13.751      0.000       1.117      1.489
===============================================================================
Omnibus:                      298.087   Durbin-Watson:                  2.017
Prob(Omnibus):                  0.000   Jarque-Bera (JB):            3616.004
Skew:                           0.754   Prob(JB):                        0.00
Kurtosis:                      11.239   Cond. No.                        1.07
===============================================================================
```

The coefficient for variable **Mkt - RF** is the estimated β for Tesla, Inc. Here we see that Tesla's β is 1.3029. It has a higher market risk than the market portfolio, which is not surprising for a new tech company.

16.3 Fama and French Three-Factor Model

The CAPM regression is simple regression, having only one explanatory variable. The function **sm.OLS( )** can do multiple regression, too. Let's look at the Fama and French Three-Factor Model (FF) to understand regressing on multiple independent variables.

Because FF is often used to test whether a well diversified portfolio has excess to their risk-adjusted returns, let's work on a portfolio, instead of an individual stock like Tesla. Please go to Yahoo! Finance® to download the daily record for iShares® Core S&P Mid-Cap ETF (IJH), one of the largest ETFs traded.

For the FF regression, you only need to change TSLA to IJH in Line 5, 6, and 7, in addition to modifying your right-hand-side variable (Line 10) as

x = data[["Mkt-RF", "SMB", "HML"]]

```
                          OLS Regression Results
==============================================================================
Dep. Variable:                      y   R-squared:                      0.941
Model:                            OLS   Adj. R-squared:                 0.941
Method:                   Least Squares   F-statistic:                2.309e+04
Date:                Wed, 21 Mar 2018   Prob (F-statistic):              0.00
Time:                        14:44:50   Log-Likelihood:               -1261.8
No. Observations:                4363   AIC:                            2532.
Df Residuals:                    4359   BIC:                            2557.
Df Model:                           3
Covariance Type:            nonrobust
==============================================================================
                 coef    std err          t      P>|t|      [95.0% Conf. Int.]
------------------------------------------------------------------------------
const          0.0063      0.005      1.279      0.201      -0.003      0.016
Mkt-RF         1.0121      0.004    248.186      0.000       1.004      1.020
SMB            0.3821      0.009     44.668      0.000       0.365      0.399
HML            0.1097      0.008     14.500      0.000       0.095      0.125
==============================================================================
Omnibus:                      497.792   Durbin-Watson:                  2.296
Prob(Omnibus):                  0.000   Jarque-Bera (JB):            3586.662
Skew:                          -0.290   Prob(JB):                        0.00
Kurtosis:                       7.404   Cond. No.                        2.21
==============================================================================
```

Because the time period of your data is unlikely to be the same as mine, your output chart will look slightly different. In the summary output above, you can read the coefficients, also known as factor loadings in the FF regression. We can observe that all three factors have explanatory power for IJH's excess return. They are both economically and statistically significant.

In the context of market efficiency, we are interested in the statistical significance of the intercept. Since the intercept term is not statistically significant, we don't see IJH to have positive risk-adjusted returns, also known as α.

16.4 Logistic Regression

A logit function transforms a linear function of independent variables into a value between 0 and 1. For a binary-outcome linear function, such value is interpreted as the probability of one of the outcomes. Specifically, the logit (logistic) regression estimates the following model:

$$y = \frac{1}{1 + e^{-(\alpha + \beta_1 x_1 + \beta_2 x_2 \ldots + \epsilon)}},$$

where y takes only 0 and 1 and x's are explanatory variables.

Let's use a rather silly example to illustrate how logistic regression is conducted. Download from the book's website logit.csv. It contains annual stock market performance, calculated from Prof. Ken French's data, and the average January temperature in Central Park, obtained from National Weather Service. In the stock performance record, I only have the value as **1** when the market in that particular year is up, and **0** when down.

The explanatory variables have only the temperature in Fahrenheit and a constant term. The regression is done through the following code.

```
01 import statsmodels.api as sm
02 import pandas as pd
03
04 data = pd.read_csv('logit.csv',index_col=0)
05
06 data['Intercept'] = 1
07
08 logit = sm.Logit(data['Up'], data.iloc[:, 1:3]).fit( )
09 print(logit.summary( ))
```

The way in Python to run logistic regression is similar to how we run OLS. We just replace **sm.OLS** with **sm.Logit**.

```
                         Logit Regression Results
==============================================================================
Dep. Variable:                     Up   No. Observations:                   55
Model:                          Logit   Df Residuals:                       53
Method:                           MLE   Df Model:                            1
Date:                Wed, 21 Mar 2018   Pseudo R-squ.:                  0.01761
Time:                        18:17:01   Log-Likelihood:                 -28.345
converged:                       True   LL-Null:                        -28.853
                                        LLR p-value:                     0.3134
==============================================================================
                 coef    std err          z      P>|z|      [95.0% Conf. Int.]
------------------------------------------------------------------------------
Temperature    0.0757      0.076      0.998      0.318      -0.073       0.224
Intercept     -1.1553      2.429     -0.476      0.634      -5.916       3.605
==============================================================================
```

From the regression output, we can construct the estimated model as

$$\text{Probability of an up year} = \frac{1}{1 + e^{1.1553 - 0.0757 Temp}}.$$

The model predicts that a hotter January in Central Park leads to a bullish market. This result is from the sign of the coefficient.

The model also predicts that with an average January temperature of 10 degrees in Central Park, the stock market has only 40% chance of having an up year. Of course, this is a silly model without any economic meaning. It doesn't have statistical meanings as well, because the z values are too big.

16.5   Exercises

Questions with asterisks have sample solutions on the book's website (www.csandaa.com/python-book).

1.* β with monthly prices. When estimating $\beta's$, the industry practice is to work on monthly returns. Let's also do that. Download the monthly csv file for **Fama/French 3 Factors**[1]. Run OLS regression to estimate Tesla, Inc.'s β.

You will need to massage the data before merging the two files. Because Ken French's monthly factors are not indexed in the date format that pandas can recognize, we need to convert the dates first. Implement the following code before merging.

```
01 import datetime as dt
02 french_m = pd.read_csv("french_m.csv", index_col=0)
03 ind = [ ]
04 for i in range(len(french_m)):
05      x = french_m.index[i]
06      ind.append(dt.datetime(x//100, x%100, 1))
07 french_m.index = ind
08 tsla = pd.read_csv("TSLA.csv",parse_dates=True, index_col=0)
09 tsla = tsla.resample("MS").last( ) #MS means start of the month
```

2. Rolling regression. Stocks are not rigid blocks. Management, competition and regulatory environment often change their systematic risks. In other words, $\beta's$ are not stable over time. We can see the changes of a stock's β over time by doing rolling regression.

   (a) Let's use Tesla's daily record for this exercise. Use only the first 500 dates' trading records to run the CAPM regression.

   (b) Convert part (a) into a for loop to run rolling regression, using 500 days as the regression window. Store the estimated $\beta's$ in a list called **beta**. Use the last day of each 500 day window as the corresponding date for the $\beta's$. You can store **data.index[ ]** in another list called **date**.

   (c) Create a DataFrame by making the two lists in part (b) into a dictionary. Then plot the β series over time. What do you see? Some useful hints to create the DataFrame object.

```
01 rolling = pd.DataFrame({"date": date, "beta": beta})
02 rolling = rolling.set_index("date")
03 rolling["beta"].plot( )
```

3. Explain the market with a variable from FRED. FRED is the data aggregator maintained by the St.Louis Federal Reserve Bank. It has an extensive collection of economic indicators. Let's try to use one economic variable to explain the market's performance.

   (a) Search in FRED for the civilian unemployment rate (UNRATE). Download the series' csv file into your working directory.

   Alternatively, you can employ the **pandas_datareader** library to grab data from FRED.

---

[1]This file contains both monthly and annual factors. Delete annual factors before importing to Python.

```
01 import pandas_datareader as web
02 import datetime
03 start = datetime.datetime(1948, 1, 1)
04 end = datetime.datetime(2017, 9, 30)
05 unrate = web.DataReader("UNRATE", "fred", start, end)
```

(b) Next, go to Yahoo! Finance to download the daily record of the ETF SPY. Make sure you use Line 09 in Exercise 1 to re-sample your daily record to monthly.

(c) Estimate the following model. $R_{SPY} = \alpha + \beta \times UNRATE + \epsilon$.
   Interpret the result.

4.* Testing the CAPM. A conclusion of the CAPM is that stocks with higher systematic risks, proxied by the β, should have higher expected return. If we can plot various stocks' expected returns against their $\beta's$, we should observe an upward sloping straight line, provided the CAPM is valid.

(a) Use the **pandas_datareader** library to get stock prices from Google Finance. We will use the component stocks in the S&P 500®. Please refer to Exercise 1 in Chapter 15 for this step.

(b) Once you have downloaded the component stocks' prices, find their respective average returns. Store these average returns in a list.

(c) Also run the CAPM regression on **all** component stocks. Store the estimated $\beta's$ in another list.

(d) Combine the two lists in part (b) and (c) to create a DataFrame. Then plot returns vs. $\beta's$. Is the CAPM alive or dead in your data?

Chapter 17

Time Series Fitting

Most financial data are time series. Fitting financial data with time series models to understand the data is common practice in the industry. Python has plenty of built-in functions to take care of time series models.

17.1 An AR Model with statsmodels.tsa

Let me illustrate how to estimate time series models with a simple autoregressive, one-period lag model. The so-called **AR(1)** model can be written as

$$R_t = \alpha + \beta \times R_{t-1} + \epsilon_t.$$

Our example is still based on Tesla's daily records. Try the following code.

```
01 import statsmodels.tsa.api as sm #The library name is different from last chapter.
02 import pandas as pd
03
04 data = pd.read_csv("TSLA_d.csv", parse_dates=True, index_col=0)
05 data["Return"] = data["Adj Close"].pct_change( )
06 data = data.dropna( )
07 result = sm.ARMA(data["Return"], (1, 0)).fit( )
08 print(result.summary( ))
```

Note that the AR process is part of a bigger ARMA (autoregressive moving average) model family. Estimating an AR(1) model is the same thing as estimating an ARMA model with AR polynomial lag of 1 and MA lag of 0. This is why we apply the **ARMA** function in line 7. For data series **y** fitted with ARMA(p, q), the function is called by sm.ARMA(y, (p, q)).

```
                              ARMA Model Results
==============================================================================
Dep. Variable:                 Return   No. Observations:                1237
Model:                      ARMA(1, 0)   Log Likelihood               2376.137
Method:                        css-mle   S.D. of innovations             0.035
Date:                 Mon, 26 Mar 2018   AIC                         -4746.275
Time:                         22:54:35   BIC                         -4730.914
Sample:                     06-30-2010   HQIC                        -4740.497
                           - 05-29-2015
==============================================================================
                 coef    std err          z      P>|z|      [95.0% Conf. Int.]
------------------------------------------------------------------------------
const          0.0025      0.001      2.490      0.013       0.001      0.005
ar.L1.Return   0.0057      0.028      0.202      0.840      -0.050      0.061
                                  Roots
==============================================================================
                 Real           Imaginary           Modulus         Frequency
------------------------------------------------------------------------------
AR.1           174.4572           +0.0000j          174.4572           0.0000
------------------------------------------------------------------------------
```

It's not surprising that the stock return series does not follow a simple autoregressive model. The lag term's coefficient is not statistically significant. Just imagine how many traders would have piled on these findings, if they were statistically significant. But it serves the purpose of helping us understand time series model fitting.

17.2   Autocorrelation Functions

But we are getting ahead of ourselves. For serious time series model fitting, we need to check stationarity of the data first. The statistical meaning of stationarity can be understood as data having long-run equilibria in both its level and volatility. Regression of non-stationary data can only find a spurious relationship that bears little importance in interpretation.

Stock prices are usually believed to be non-stationary. But after we take differences of prices to create the return series, we transform non-stationary data to stationary ones.

There are various ways to check stationarity. The autocorrelation functions (ACF) I am going to introduce are one of them.

For a univariate series y_t, the correlation ρ between two observations, separated by s periods, can be written into a function of s. For a stationary series, the further away in time of the two $y's$, the smaller the autocorrelation. Therefore a decaying ACF that converges to zero geometrically indicates stationarity of the data.

The library statsmodels has a built-in **sm.acf( )** function that can calculate ACF of any univariate series. Let's use Tesla's daily records as an example.

```
09 import matplotlib.pyplot as plt
10 acf1 = sm.acf(data["Adj Close"], nlags = 10)
11 plt.bar(range(len(acf1)), acf1)
```

```
12 plt.xlabel("Lags")
13 plt.title("ACF of Tesla Prices")
```

Line 10 calls sm.acf( ). In the second argument of the function, we pick 10 as the number of lags. The output graph is shown below.

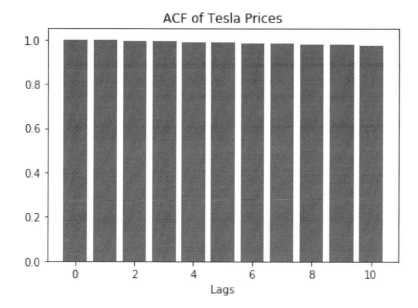

As we can see in the ACF graph, the autocorrelation does not seem to decay as the number of lags increases. It will be a different story when we turn to the return series in the next block of code.

```
14 acf2 = sm.acf(data["Return"], nlags = 10)
15 plt.figure( )
16 plt.bar(range(len(acf2)), acf2)
17 plt.xlabel("Lags")
18 plt.title("ACF of Tesla Returns")
```

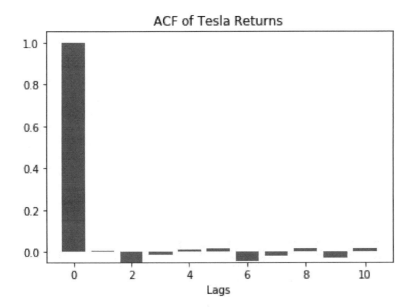

The decay happens fast. It's unambiguous that the return series appear to be "more stationary" than the price series.

17.3 Augmented Dickey-Fuller Test for Unit Root

The stationarity test is often related to an important hypothesis in finance: whether stock prices follow a random walk process. The random walk hypothesis is to describe the movement of a stock's price the same way as a drunkard wandering at night. The drunkard's movement is totally random, but if he is pushed to a certain direction, he will not resist it. In other words, prices are unpredictable, but have memory.

If a data generating process is random walk, it is non-stationary and also known to have a unit root. To test whether the process contains a unit root, researchers often look at the following model:

$y_t = a_0 + a_1 y_{t-1} + \epsilon_t,$
where y_t is the price level at time t, the error term ϵ_t is referred to as noise or innovation (see how economists mix up two orthogonal words together?) and a_0 is a drift term (you think of it as a natural trend of stock prices.)

The coefficient we are interested in is a_1, but to test the unit root hypothesis, we often write the equation as

$y_t - y_{t-1} = a_0 + (a_1 - 1)y_{t-1} + \epsilon_t.$

Or

$$\Delta y_t = a_0 + \gamma y_{t-1} + \epsilon_t.$$

If y_t has a unit root, a_1 should be no different from one and γ zero. In other words, if we cannot show γ is statistically different from zero, we cannot reject the null hypothesis that y_t has a unit root. This test was called the Dickey-Fuller test (Dickey and Fuller, 1979).

The library statsmodels has a built-in function **adfuller( )** to implement the Dickey-Fuller test. Let's continue with our Tesla example. Try these lines.

```
19 df = sm.adfuller(data["Adj Close"]), regression = 'c')
20 print(df)
```

The output is a tuple of numbers:

(-0.053195331585549219, 0.95390547395442615, 0, 1236, {'1%': -3.4356517256484151, '5%': -2.8638812231195359, '10%': -2.5680164989107781}, 6776.8222635617267)

The first number is the test statistics. Comparing it to the critical values from Dickey and Fuller (1979) (listed as a dict in the output, with 1%, 5%, and 10% thresholds), we find that it is not larger in absolute value than even the 10% threshold. Then we know that we cannot reject the random walk null hypothesis. The second value in the output is the p-value, which confirms out conclusion.

Try using Tesla's return series for the Dickey-Fuller test. You should be able to reject the random walk null hypothesis without any difficulties.

When I use the sm.adfuller( ) function, I supply only two parameters: the variable in question and **regression = 'c'**. This second argument can be taken from a dict {'c', 'ct', 'ctt', 'nc'}. With only 'c', we are testing the model with a drift. If we use 'ct', we add a time trend to the model, in addition to the drift. With daily record in use, I don't see a strong argument to add the time trend for the hypothesis testing.

If you pay attention to the function name, you see that it is actually called augmented Dickey-Fuller test. This is to account for the possible autocorrelation of the data series. We "augment" the model with lag variables. Specifically, we should be testing

$$y_t = a_0 + a_1 y_{t-1} + a_2 y_{t-2} + a_3 y_{t-3} + \ldots\ldots + \epsilon_t;$$

Or,

$$\Delta y_t = a_0 + \gamma y_{t-1} + \beta_2 \Delta y_{t-2} + \beta_3 \Delta y_{t-3} + \ldots\ldots + \epsilon_t.$$

γ is still the coefficient we are interested in. We often use either AIC (Akaike Information Criterion) or BIC (Bayesian Information Criterion) to select the number of lags. For example,

21 adf = sm.adfuller(data["Adj Close"]), regression = 'c', autolag = 'BIC')
22 print(adf)

The third argument in sm.adfuller( ) is to pick the method to select the number of lags. You can try 'AIC' or 't-stat' as an alternative. The output also tells us that we cannot reject the unit root hypothesis:

(-0.053195331585549219, 0.95390547395442615, 0, 1236, {'1%':
-3.4356517256484151, '5%': -2.8638812231195359,
'10%': -2.5680164989107781}, 6787.023967379615)

17.4   ARIMA

Many non-stationary series can be converted into stationary data by taking first- or second-order differences. These are called difference-stationary data. Since it is a simple step for the econometrician to difference data series, it is convenient to use a more comprehensive model family called ARIMA to encompass both stationary and non-stationary data.

A series is said to be fitted with the ARIMA(p, d, q) model. The notation **p** is the lag number of autoregressive terms, **d** the number of differences, and **q** the lag number of moving average terms.

Recall in lines 7-8, we fit Tesla's return series with an AR(1) model. It is the same as fitting an ARIMA(1, 0, 0) model. Try

23 arima = sm.ARIMA(data["Return"], order = (1, 0, 0)).fit( )
24 print(arima.summary( ))

You should have identical result to what we observe in Section 17.1.

What we frequently see in an ARIMA model is to have a first-differenced series, i.e. ARIMA(p, 1, q). In general, the variable in question is now

$$c_t = y_t - y_{t-1}.$$

The rest of the model specification is the same as an ARMA(p, q) model.

17.5   Model Selection

Box and Jenkins (1976) formulate a procedure to select a time series model. Let's walk through this classic method to fit a model to an exchange rate data series.

Go to the book's website to download DEXJPUS.csv to your working directory. The file contains daily exchange rates between the Japanese yen and U.S. dollar. The data source is the Board of

Governors of the Federal Reserve System via the Federal Reserve Bank of St. Louis. The numbers in the file tell you how many yens a dollar can buy. First, we should "look at" the data.

```
01 import pandas as pd
02 import numpy as np
03 import matplotlib.pyplot as plt
04
05 data = pd.read_csv("DEXJPUS.csv", parse_dates=True, index_col = 0)
06 data["LogP"] = 0
07 for i in range(len(data)-1):
08      data.iloc[i, 1] = np.log(data.iloc[i+1, 0])-np.log(data.iloc[i, 0])
09 data = data.dropna( )
10
11 data["DEXJPUS"].plot( )
12 plt.figure( )
13 data["LogP"].plot( )
```

The code generates two graphs. The first one is the exchange rate and shows its non-stationarity. The second one is the differenced series. Here I use the log price difference, which is the common practice for differencing a series in finance. The interpretations for straightforward returns and log price differences are slightly different, but log normal distribution is a much better description of financial data than assuming returns to be normally distributed. In any case, the characteristics of the two series in time series model fitting are identical.

We can observe stationarity much better in the second graph.

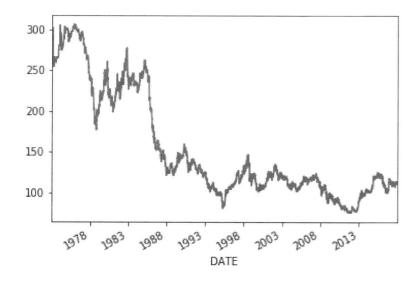

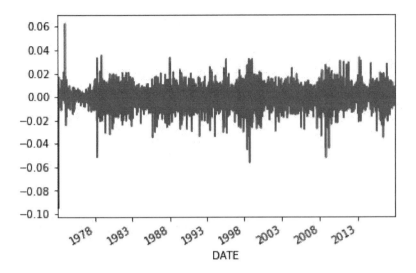

Our next job is to use ACF to "seriously look" at the exchange rate return's stationarity.

```
14 import statsmodels.tsa.api as sm
15 acf = sm.acf(data["LogP"], nlags=10)
16 plt.bar(range(len(acf)), acf)
17 plt.xlabel("Lags")
18 plt.title("ACF of Log Yen/Dollar")
```

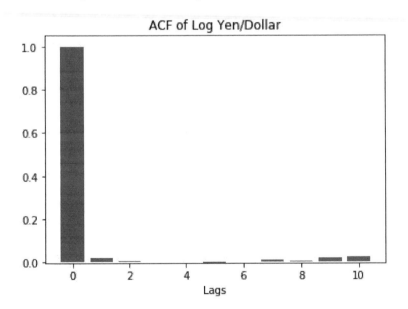

1, 7, 9, and 10 lags show a slight possibility of autocorrlation, but not terribly significant.

Now let's fit an ARMA model to the log exchange rate. We will use AIC and BIC to select the model.

```
19 order =[(1,0), (2,0), (1,1), (2,1), (2,2)] #Set up ARMA(p, q) lag order.
20
21 AIC = [ ]
22 BIC = [ ]
23 lag = [ ]
24
25 for i in order:
26        result = sm.ARMA(data["LogP"], i).fit( )
27        AIC.append(result.aic)
28        BIC.append(result.bic)
29
30 model = pd.DataFrame(AIC, index= None, columns = ["AIC"])
31 model["BIC"] = BIC
32 model["Lag"] = order
33 print(model)
```

The result is a DataFrame object:

	AIC	BIC	Lag
0	-81408.467516	-81386.470373	(1, 0)
1	-81406.688352	-81377.358828	(2, 0)
2	-81406.738270	-81377.408746	(1, 1)
3	-81404.685760	-81368.023855	(2, 1)
4	-81402.777099	-81358.782813	(2, 2)

Both AIC and BIC indicate that an ARMA(1, 0) model is the best among the five choices. Let's further run a diagnostic check on ARMA(1, 0).

```
34 arma = sm.ARMA(data["LogP"],(1,0)).fit( )
35 acf = sm.acf(arma.resid, nlags=10)
36 plt.bar(range(len(acf)), acf)
37 plt.xlabel("Lags")
38 plt.title("ARMA(1,0) Residual ACF")
```

The result is a plot of residuals for the fitted model.

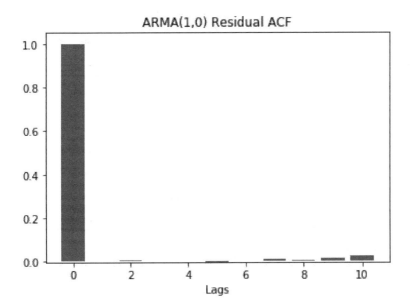

It is hard to detect serial correlations in the residuals. In case you are interested of the Q-statistics, none of the Q's show that we can reject the null hypothesis that the residuals are serially correlated: $Q(1) = 0.00010009457986875504$, $Q(5) = 0.39424059672110978$, and $Q(10) = 12.791663187929931$.

17.6   Forecast and Forecast Errors

We use model fitting results to either explain things that happened in the past or to forecast things about to happen. In finance, many of us ultimately hope that we can build a valid model to predict financial asset movements. But how do we know a model is really good for the task?

To answer that question, I need to introduce the concept of out-of-sample forecasting. When we looked at fitted values and realized observations in our data, we were conducting an in-sample forecast. This is alright for estimating model parameters, but not ideal for predicting "the future". This is because you inevitably use results from the future to build your model.

The better way is to estimate the model and take the results to the future for testing. In finance, this is only done by people who brazenly believe their models are superior without supporting evidence. We often resort to the second best solution–out-of-sample forecasting. The way to do it is to break historical data into two or more sub-samples. We then use the older part to estimate the model and then bring the model to the second half of the sample that acts as observations in the future.

Let me use the yen/dollar exchange rate's ARMA(1, 0) model to show you how out-of-sample forecasting works.

```
01 import pandas as pd
02 import numpy as np
```

```
03 import statsmodels.tsa.api as sm
04
05 data = pd.read_csv("DEXJPUS.csv", parse_dates=True, index_col = 0)
06 data["LogP"] = 0
07 for i in range(len(data)-1):
08     data.iloc[i, 1] = np.log(data.iloc[i+1, 0])-np.log(data.iloc[i, 0])
09 data = data.dropna( )
10
11 h = len(data)//2 #Find the midpoint to split the data.
12 half = data.iloc[0 : h, :]
13 arma = sm.ARMA(half["LogP"],(1,0)).fit( ) #Estimate with half of sample.
14
15 data["Forecast"] = 0
16 for i in range(len(data)-1):
17     data.iloc[i+1, 2] = arma.params[0]+arma.params[1]*data.iloc[i, 1]
```

Here arma.params[0] and arma.params[1] extract the constant and coefficent of the model.
We can certainly compare the forecast series and the realized. But without a benchmark to compare to, we cannot really say how good the model is. The benchmark frequently used is the random walk model. Even if you don't believe in market efficiency, it still serves as a relevant benchmark.

```
18 data["FP"] = 0
19 for i in range(len(data)-1):
20     data.iloc[i+1, 3] = np.exp(np.log(data.iloc[i, 0])+data.iloc[i, 2])
21
22 data["RW"] = 0
23 for i in range(len(data)-1):
24 data.iloc[i+1, 4] = data.iloc[i, 0]
```

Lines 19-20 need some explanations. The new column **FP** is the forecast exchange rate, which is deduced from the forecast log price difference.

For the random walk model, an intuitive way to look at it is that the best guess of tomorrow's price is today's. Lines 22-24 simply implements such an idea. Now we can look at the forecast work we have done so far.

In [0]: data.loc["2017/1/5": "2017/1/10"]
Out [0]:

DATE	DEXJPUS	LogP	Forecast	FP	RW
2017-01-05	115.46	0.011967	-0.000955	117.340863	117.38
2017-01-06	116.85	-0.006698	0.000314	115.349830	115.46
2017-01-09	116.07	-0.002847	-0.000518	116.886640	116.85
2017-01-10	115.74	0.004483	-0.000347	116.009870	116.07

Essentially, we want to run a horse race between columns FP and RW. To measure the prediction accuracy, we compare their **Mean Squared Errors (MSE)**. MSE is defined as

$$MSE = \frac{1}{T}\sum_{i=1}^{T}(\hat{y}_i - y_i)^2,$$

where T is the number of observations, $\hat{y}_i$ the forecast value and y_i the realized one. The following code block shows how to calculate MSE.

```
25 MSE1 = 0 #Initiate MSE for model forecast.
26 MSE2 = 0 #Initiate MSE for random walk.
27
28 for i in range(h, len(data)): #h is the midpoint of the data.
29      MSE1 += (data.iloc[i, 3] - data.iloc[i, 0])**2
30      MSE2 += (data.iloc[i, 4] - data.iloc[i, 0])**2
31
32 print("Forecast MSE =", MSE1/h)
33 print("Random Walk MSE =", MSE2/h)
```

The result is

Forecast MSE = 0.575860775203
Random Walk MSE = 0.574445176137

We have clear evidence that a simple AR(1) model cannot beat random walk in this data.

17.7   Exercises

Questions with asterisks have sample solutions on the book's website (www.csandaa.com/python-book).

1. Fit an AR(1) model to the Tesla daily return series.

    (a) Use the full sample data for estimating the model. Report the estimation result.
    (b) Use the first half of the data to fit the model. Report the estimation result. Create a forecast price series for the second half of the data.
    (c) Continue with (b). Produce a Random Walk series out of Tesla's price series.
    (d) Compare the forecast errors of the models in (b) and (c), using Mean Squared Errors. Which model has a smaller MSE?

2.* Go to the Federal Reserve Bank of St. Louis's website to download the Real Gross GDP series of the U.S. (GDPC1). Apply the ADF test to determine whether the series has a unit root.

3. Rolling estimations. Continue with DEXJPUS.csv in the main text. Instead of breaking the sample data into two periods. Let's do rolling estimations. Use 2-year's window to estimate an AR(1) model fitted to the exchange rate data. Plot the coefficients over time.

4.* Use Box-Jenkins method to select and fit a time series model to the Treasury Term Premia estimate series. The data is on the Federal Reserve Bank of New York's website. Once download the data, use the series called ACMY10.

5. Use Box-Jenkins method to select and fit a time series model to the TIPS. TIPS is the 10-Year Treasury Inflation-Index Security. You can get the data from the Federal Reserve Bank of St. Louis's database. Use series code: DFII10.

Chapter 18

Optimization

Optimization often means to find a maximum or minimum value given certain constraints. In the real world, it is rarely possible to find analytical solutions for maximization or minimization problems. We have to rely on numerical solutions.

There are plenty of methods of finding acceptable optimal solutions. Many of them are beyond the scope of this introductory text. But the few examples we will do can show you the power of Python programming.

18.1   A Four-Asset Portfolio

In Exercise 7 of Chapter 8, we introduce the two-asset portfolio, which helps illustrate how portfolio managers build portfolios. In reality, the optimal portfolio is constructed with many assets. Inclusion of a large number of assets in a portfolio complicates the calculation. We will need to employ linear algebra for that. However, we can use a four-asset portfolio as an example to see how optimization can be implemented in Python. For the general case of N assets, please see Exercise 2 in the end of this chapter.

A four-asset portfolio can be described by

$r_p = x_1 r_1 + x_2 r_2 + x_3 r_3 + x_4 r_4;$

$\sigma_p^2 = x_1^2 \sigma_1^2 + x_2^2 \sigma_2^2 + x_3^2 \sigma_3^2 + x_4^2 \sigma_4^2 + 2x_1 x_2 \sigma_1 \sigma_2 \rho_{12} + 2x_1 x_3 \sigma_1 \sigma_3 \rho_{13} + 2x_1 x_4 \sigma_1 \sigma_4 \rho_{14} + 2x_2 x_3 \sigma_2 \sigma_3 \rho_{23} + 2x_2 x_4 \sigma_2 \sigma_4 \rho_{24} + 2x_3 x_4 \sigma_3 \sigma_4 \rho_{34},$

where x_i is the fraction of wealth allocation for asset i, r_i the expected return of asset i, σ_i^2 the variance of asset i's return, and ρ_{ij} the correlation coefficient between assets i and j.

The parameters[1] we are going to use are $r_1 = .003$, $r_2 = .036$, $r_3 = .013$, $r_4 = .015$, $\sigma_1 = .042$,

---

[1] I select four stocks for a five-year period to obtain these parameters. They are XOM, FB, BMY, and COF.

$\sigma_2 = .089$, $\sigma_3 = .071$, $\sigma_4 = .060$ $\rho_{12} = -.090$, $\rho_{13} = .332$, $\rho_{14} = .400$, $\rho_{23} = -.142$, $\rho_{24} = .104$ and $\rho_{34} = .219$.

The following lines of code create 100,000 portfolios by randoming allocating weights of investment to assets **1**, **2**, **3**, and **4**.

```
01 import random
02 import matplotlib.pyplot as plt
03 def xlist(n): #Define a function to randomly form portfolios
04       x = [ ]
05       for i in range(n):
06             x.append(random.random( ))
07       return [j/sum(x) for j in x] #Note the square bracket here².
08
09 def port(x1, x2, x3, x4, r1, r2, r3, r4, sig1, sig2, sig3, sig4,
10       rho12, rho13, rho14, rho23, rho24, rho34):
11       #Define a function to Calculate portfolio returns and sigmas³.
12       port_ret = x1*r1 + x2*r2 + x3*r3 + x4*r4
13       port_sig =
14       (x1**2*sig1**2+x2**2*sig2**2+x3**2*sig3**2+x4**2*sig4**2
15       +2*x1*x2*sig1*sig2*rho12+2*x1*x3*sig1*sig3*rho13
16       +2*x1*x4*sig1*sig4*rho14+2*x2*x3*sig2*sig3*rho23
17       +2*x2*x4*sig2*sig4*rho24+2*x3*x4*sig3*sig4*rho34)**.5
18       return [port_ret, port_sig]
19
20 r1 = .003
21 r2 = .036
22 r3 = .013
23 r4 = .015
24 sig1 = .042
25 sig2 = .089
26 sig3 = .071
27 sig4 = .06
28 rho12 = -.090
29 rho13 = .332
30 rho14 = .4
31 rho23 = -.141
32 rho24 = .104
33 rho34 = .219
34
35 x = [ ] #Lists for portfolio outputs: x is sigma, y return, and portlist the compositions.
36 y = [ ]
37 portlist = [ ]
38
```

---

[2]This is a list literal (generator) with a quick for loop.

[3]A trick is used here: For a long line, you can break it into two but enclose them in one parenthesis.

```
39 for i in range(100000):
40      [x1, x2, x3, x4] = xlist(4)
41      portlist.append([x1, x2, x3, x4])
42      portfolio = port(x1, x2, x3, x4, r1, r2, r3, r4, sig1, sig2, sig3, sig4,
43      rho12, rho13, rho14, rho23, rho24)
44      x.append(portfolio[1])
45      y.append(portfolio[0])
46
47 plt.plot(x, y,"b.") #Let's plot the Efficient Frontier.
48 plt.xlabel("Sigma")
49 plt.ylabel("Return")
```

As can be seen in the graphic output, these 100,000 portfolios cover a wide swath of possibilities.

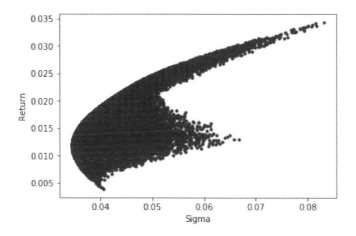

The outer edge of the colored area is the Efficient Frontier. For the portfolio manager, the job is to find portfolios on the Efficient Frontier, because these are superior to those inside the Frontier. To construct the Efficient Frontier, however, we need an optimization algorithm.

The optimization process is not ONE optimization problem, but many. In fact, we turn the question around by first requiring a portfolio to have a certain amount of return, say .01. We then find the portfolio with the **smallest** variance possible, given the specified return. Repeating the process with different levels of returns, we can construct the whole frontier. The optimization process here, in other words, is to find the minimum value of return variance for these portfolios.

I will introduce two ways to accomplish this task.

18.2 Brute Force Grid Search

We will take the 100,000 portfolios as given and search within these. In a sense, this is optimization done with Monte Carlo simulation.

The algorithm is to first sort the 100,000 portfolios by their returns and then divide them into 100 groups. In each group, we find the portfolio with the smallest variance and then report its composition.

```
48 import pandas as pd
49 data = pd.DataFrame("Return" : y , "Sigma" :x , "Portfolio": portlist)
50 data = data.sort_values(by="Return")
51 data = data.reset_index( ) #Reset the index for using the .ix method later.
51 del data["index"] #Delete the redundant index column.
52
53 xx = [ ] #Lists for the EF outputs: xx is sigma, yy return, and ef the compositions.
54 yy = [ ]
55 ef = [ ]
56
57 for i in range(100):
58      subset = data.ix[i*1000:i*1000+999, :]
59      subset = subset.reset_index( )
60      del subset["index"]
61      for j in range(len(subset)):
62          if subset.ix[j,2] == min(subset["Sigma"]):
63              xx.append(subset.ix[j,2])
64              yy.append(subset.ix[j,1])
65              ef.append(subset.ix[j,0])
66
67 plt.plot(xx, yy, "k.")
68 plt.xlabel("Sigma")
69 plt.ylabel("Return")
```

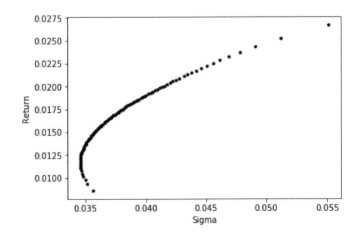

18.3 Optimization with Scipy

Given a desired rate of return of the portfolio, we can find the optimal portfolio by minimizing its variance. Python's **scipy** library has a built-in minimizer for such a task. Before I show the code to implement the algorithm, let's understand how an optimization problem is framed mathematically.

$$\min_{x_1, x_2 \dots, x_N} \sigma_p^2$$

$$s.t. \ x_1 + x_2 + x_3 + \cdots + x_N = 1;$$

$$x_1 r_1 + x_2 r_2 + \cdots + x_N r_N = \bar{r},$$

where $\bar{r}$ is the specified rate of return.

In a nutshell, we need to tell an optimizer the objective function and the constraints. Here is sample code of how to implement the **minimize** function from **scipy.optimize** library.

```
01 from scipy.optimize import minimize
02 import matplotlib.pyplot as plt
03
04 def port(x):  #This is the objective function.
05        #We modify port( ) from the previous section; weights as x, a list.
06        x1 = x[0]
07        x2 = x[1]
08        x3 = x[2]
09        x4 = x[3]
10        sig1 = .042
11        sig2 = .089
12        sig3 = .071
13        sig4 = .06
14        rho12 = -.090
15        rho13 = .332
16        rho14 = .4
17        rho23 = -.141
18        rho24 = .104
19        rho34 = .219
20        port_sig =
21        (x1**2*sig1**2 + x2**2*sig2**2 + x3**2*sig3**2 + x4**2*sig4**2
22        + 2*x1*x2*sig1*sig2*rho12 + 2*x1*x3*sig1*sig3*rho13
23        + 2*x1*x4*sig1*sig4*rho14 + 2*x2*x3*sig2*sig3*rho23
24        + 2*x2*x4*sig2*sig4*rho24 + 2*x3*x4*sig3*sig4*rho34)**.5
25        return port_sig
26
27 r1 = .003
28 r2 = .036
29 r3 = .013
30 r4 = .015
```

```
31
32 def budget(x):#Define constraint 1 as a function.
33       y = x[0] + x[1] + x[2] + x[3] -1
34       #Note that we move the right-hand-side to the left to make it a function.
35       return y
36
37 def req_return(x):#Define constraint 2 as a function.
38       ret = x[0]*r1+x[1]*r2+x[2]*r3+x[3]*r4 - port_ret
39       return ret
40
41 x = [ ]#Create lists to store portfolio outputs. x is sigma, y is return, and portlist is the com-
positions.
42 y = [ ]
43 portlist = [ ]
44
45 for i in range(100):
46       x0 = [.25, .25, .25, .25]
47       port_ret = .003+i/3000
48       #To determine the range of returns, some trials and errors are involved.
49       cons = ('type': 'eq', 'fun': budget, 'type': 'eq', 'fun': req_return)
50       bnds = ((0, None), (0, None), (0, None), (0, None))
51       result = minimize(port, x0, method = "SLSQP",
52       constraints = cons, bounds = bnds)
53       portlist.append(result.x)
54       y.append(port_ret)
55       x.append(port(result.x))
56
57 plt.plot(x, y, 'k.')
```

The code inside the for loop needs quite a few explanations. The loop repeats a hundred times. It means we solve the optimization problem exactly one hundred times.

The function **minimize( )** first takes in the objective function (**port( )** here). The second argument is the initial guess of the optimal solution. I keep it simple by supplying an equal weight portfolio as in line 46.

The third argument is the algorithm the **minimize( )** function uses to find the optimum. The function has over a dozen built-in algorithms. **SLSQP**[4] is proven to work the wonder for us.

Then the function takes the constraints written in functions. To make things easier, you should keep the inputs to the constraints and the objective function identical and write the argument in the same way as I present here. Note that I also impose boundary limitations on the weights, as you see in **bnds** in line 50. I restrict the **x's** to be non-negative.

---

[4]You really have no need or incentives to know what is inside the blackbox right now, but if you are interested, go to SciPy.org to read the documentation for **scipy.optimize.minimize**.

The graphic output (not shown here) is indistinguishable from the Efficient Frontier we produced in 18.2. It's amazing that Monte Carlo simulation is as accurate as the hard-core optimization.

18.4 Exercises

Questions with asterisks have sample solutions on the book's website (www.csandaa.com/python-book).

1. Five assets. Redo the brute force search in the main text, but include numbers from a fifth asset **WMT**. All the parameters you need are listed here.

$r_1 = .003$, $r_2 = .036$, $r_3 = .013$, $r_4 = .015$, $r_5 = .009$;

$\sigma_1 = .042$, $\sigma_2 = .089$, $\sigma_3 = .071$, $\sigma_4 = .060$, $\sigma_5 = .048$;

$\rho_{12} = -.090$, $\rho_{13} = .332$, $\rho_{14} = .400$, $\rho_{15} = .006$, $\rho_{23} = -.142$, $\rho_{24} = .104$, $\rho_{25} = -.008$, $\rho_{34} = .219$, $\rho_{35} = .008$, and $\rho_{45} = -.056$.

(a) Formulas for 5-asset portfolios:

$$r_p = x_1 r_1 + x_2 r_2 + x_3 r_3 + x_4 r_4 + x_5 r_5;$$

$$\sigma_p^2 = x_1^2 \sigma_1^2 + x_2^2 \sigma_2^2 + x_3^2 \sigma_3^2 + x_4^2 \sigma_4^2 + x_5^2 \sigma_5^2 + 2x_1 x_2 \sigma_1 \sigma_2 \rho_{12} + 2x_1 x_3 \sigma_1 \sigma_3 \rho_{13} + 2x_1 x_4 \sigma_1 \sigma_4 \rho_{14} + 2x_1 x_5 \sigma_1 \sigma_5 \rho_{15} + 2x_2 x_3 \sigma_2 \sigma_3 \rho_{23} + 2x_2 x_4 \sigma_2 \sigma_4 \rho_{24} + 2x_2 x_5 \sigma_2 \sigma_5 \rho_{25} + 2x_3 x_4 \sigma_3 \sigma_4 \rho_{34} + 2x_3 x_5 \sigma_3 \sigma_5 \rho_{35} + 2x_4 x_5 \sigma_4 \sigma_5 \rho_{45}.$$

(b) In the graphic output, do you see the Efficient Frontier expand northwestward, comparing to the 4-asset portfolios?

(c) On the Efficient Frontier, the portfolio with the smallest variance is the minimum variance portfolio. Compare the minimum variance portfolios created from 4 and 5 assets.

2.* N assets. To expand our portfolio maximization problem to a general case that can accommodate N assets, we need to know some matirx operations.

(a) Variance-covariance matrix. The formula given in the main text to calculate the portfolio variance has its roots in statistics. Specifically, a portfolio's variance can be characterized by

$X \Sigma X^T$, where

X is a $1 \times N$ vector $[x_1 \ x_2 \ \ldots \ x_N]$, denoting weights on assets $1, 2, \ldots, N$, and

$$\Sigma = \begin{bmatrix} cov(1,1) & cov(1,2) & \cdots & cov(1,N) \\ cov(2,1) & cov(2,2) & \cdots & cov(2,N) \\ \vdots & \vdots & \ddots & \vdots \\ cov(N,1) & cov(N,2) & \cdots & cov(N,N) \end{bmatrix}.$$

Note that $cov(i,j) = \sigma_i \sigma_j \rho_{ij}$. Also note that $\rho_{ii} = 1$. We can rewrite the matrix as

$$\Sigma = \begin{bmatrix} \sigma_1^2 & \sigma_1\sigma_2\rho_{12} & \cdots & \sigma_1\sigma_N\rho_{1N} \\ \sigma_2\sigma_1\rho_{21} & \sigma_2^2 & \cdots & \sigma_2\sigma_N\rho_{2N} \\ \vdots & \vdots & \ddots & \vdots \\ \sigma_N\sigma_1\rho_{N1} & \sigma_N\sigma_2\rho_{N2} & \cdots & \sigma_N^2. \end{bmatrix}.$$

Σ is known as the **variance-covariance** matrix. Try the matrix multiplication $X\Sigma X^T$ with 4 assets. You should get the same formula for portfolio variance as you see in the main text.

(b) Write a user-defined function to create a variance-covariance matrix. In this **covmat( )** function, you take in the assets' standard deviations and their correlation coefficients. Specifically, standard deviations are stored in a list $\sigma = [\sigma_1, \sigma_2, ..., \sigma_N]$ and the correlation coefficients are in a reversed pyramid-like nested list
$\rho = [[\rho_{12}, \rho_{13}, ..., \rho_{1N}], [\rho_{23}, \rho_{24}, ...\rho_{2N}], ..., [\rho_{(N-1)N}]]$.

```
01 import numpy as np #Numpy's array operations are the basis of matrix algebra
   in Python.
02 def covmat(sigma, rho):
03       n = len(sigma)
04       sigma = np.matrix(sigma) #Convert a list into a matrix.
05       sigmatrix = np.dot(np.transpose(sigma), sigma)
06       #np.dot(x,y) is the matrix multiplication of x and y.
07       #This operation takes care of all the σ's in the var-covar matrix.
08       temp = np.ones([n, n]) #An N × N matrix of ones.
09       for i in range(n): #Now we will fill in the ρ's.
10            j=i+1
11            while j < n:
12                 temp[i, j] = rho[i][j-i-1]
13                 j += 1
14       rhomatrix = np.multiply(temp, np.transpose(temp))
15       #np.multiply(x,y) is element-wise multiplication of x and y.
16       #It is also called the Hadamard product.
17       varcov = np.multiply(rhomatrix, sigmatrix)
18       return varcov
```

(c) Redo the 4-asset exercise with your new **covmat( )** function. You will need to modify your **port( )** function and where you call it.

(d) Redo the 5-asset exercise with your new **covmat( )** and **port( )** functions. Look at how easy it is to move from 4 assets to 5 assets once you add linear algebra to your toolkit. After this, you won't miss the tedious steps in Exercise 1.

(e) Nobel Prize winner Harry Markowitz pioneered the concept of the Efficient Frontier in his seminal dissertation (Markowitz, 1952). His theoretical paper didn't test on any real assets, but he intended to build portfolios with 25 assets[5]. It was proven to be technically difficult in the 1950s. He settled for 9 assets in a followup study. Armed with the computing power and flexibility of Python programming, you can easily accomplish Dr. Markowitz's goal.

Let's use 25 stocks to form the Efficient Frontier. But it's a tedious job to enter all 25 assets' parameters. Luckily, Numpy can produce the variance-covariance matrix with a built-in function.

The following is a stock symbol list randomly picked from the S&P 500® Index. Download 5 years' monthly records from Yahoo! Finance® and store them in your working directory.

['CAT', 'SO', 'VNO', 'SRE', 'ZTS', 'ILMN', 'RCL', 'KIM', 'SJM','BXP','MAC', 'ETFC', 'ULTA', 'NRG', 'BK', 'GPN', 'SPGI', 'WYN', 'PDCO', 'TXT', 'EMN', 'AFL', 'LRCX', 'CHD', 'GWW']

After converting the stock prices into returns, you should use **np.cov( )** to create the variance-covariance matrix. Note that **np.cov( )** takes in a matrix (or array) of **m × n**, where **m** is the number of variables and **n** is the number of observations.

Can you conclude that the more assets you include in the portfolios, the more "efficient" they are?

3. Redo Exercise 2(c) of this chapter with the **minimize** function from **scipy.optimize**.

4.[*] OLS regression is also an optimization problem. For a simple regression model, $y = \alpha + \beta x + \epsilon$, the coefficients α and β can be estimated by minimizing the sum of squared errors (**sse**). Specifically, given estimates of α and β, the estimated error is

$\epsilon_i = y_i - \alpha - \beta \times x_i$.

After applying all the observations x_i and y_i, the sum of squared ϵ_i is known as **sse**. Then the optimization problem can be written as

$$\min_{\alpha,\beta} sse$$

(a) Write a user-defined function to calculate the sum of squared errors, given the observations of $x's$ and $y's$. Specifically, your function **sse(params)** takes in **params** = [α, β] and returns **sse**.

---

[5]This fact was revealed by Dr. Markowitz in a video interview done for the American Financial Association in 2014.

(b) To implement the optimization algorithm we learned in 18.3, we use the famous study of the relationship between Nobel laureates per capita and chocolate consumption per capita (Messerli, 2012). Let's use data from the table[6] below to estimate the model

$Nobel = \alpha + \beta \times Chocolate + \epsilon.$

Country	Nobel Laureates per 10 million	Chocolate kg per capita
USA	11.342	6.3
Switzerland	29.728	11
Germany	13.031	11.5
United Kingdom	19.945	8
France	9.541	7
Italy	3.369	3.8
Norway	24.503	8.9
Sweden	30.27	6.3

Estimate the coefficients α and β, using **scipy.optimize.minimize**.

Do you find that the countries that consume more chocolate per capita also produce more Nobel laureates per capita?

Compare your result with OLS regression we learned in Chapter 16.

---

[6]Nobel laureate numbers per 10 million people are as of 2017 and obtained from Wikipedia. Chocolate consumption (kg per captia) is from Chocosuisse. Switzerland's number is from 2016 and the rest is from 2014.

Chapter 19

Final Words

Now that you have tasted the fun and excitement of coding. You might wonder what happens next. This book might well be your first step into the coding universe. As Marc Andreessen said in the prophetic Silicon Valley manifesto, *"Software is eating the world."* Knowing how software works and is created gives you unlimited possibilities. Therefore, you should not stop coding after finishing this book. Use Python's ease of getting into coding as a stepping stone to more opportunities. Depending on the projects that you will work on, you might need to learn other languages. But you are prepared. You might struggle a little bit when you find the unfriendliness of other tools, but the idea is almost the same. Remember that Stack Overflow and Google are coders' best friends.

But Python doesn't need to be only a stepping stone. Its flexibility and vast user network have made Python a power to reckon with. The quirky but illuminating webcomic **xkcd** once showed the potential power of Python in one of its comics. In it, the protagonist is having a conversation regarding Python with a friend when flying. She is asked how she could fly. "I just typed **import antigravity**," she answered. Flying might not be as simple as importing a Python library, but for almost everything else, there is always a possibility that some other coders in the community have already built a library for that particular function. Maybe some day it will be your turn to build one of these libraries.

Thank you and code away!

Bibliography

Fischer Black and Myron Scholes. The pricing of options and corporate liabilities. *Journal of Political Economy*, 81(3):637–654, 1973.

George EP Box and Gwilym M Jenkins. *Time Series Analysis: Forecasting and Control, revised ed.* Holden-Day, 1976.

David A Dickey and Wayne A Fuller. Distribution of the estimators for autoregressive time series with a unit root. *Journal of the American statistical association*, 74(366a):427–431, 1979.

Harry Markowitz. Portfolio selection. *The Journal of Finance*, 7(1):77–91, 1952.

Wes McKinney. *Python for Data Analysis: Data Wrangling with Pandas, NumPy, and IPython.* " O'Reilly Media, Inc.", 2012.

Franz H. Messerli. Chocolate consumption, cognitive function, and nobel laureates. *The New England Journal of Medicine*, 367:16, 2012.

William F Sharpe. Capital asset prices: A theory of market equilibrium under conditions of risk. *The Journal of Finance*, 19(3):425–442, 1964.

Index

.
.append()   17
.count()   101
.DataReader()   97
.describe()   76, 91
.download()   96
.drop()   108
.dropna()   68, 75, 91, 111
.find()   16
.groupby()   100
.head()   66, 74, 99
.iloc[]   66, 75
.index[]   76
.join()   90, 111
.keys()   94
.loc[]   68, 75
.lower()   19, 36
.max()   19
.mean()   101
.median()   77
.min()   19
.pct_change()   75, 111
.plot()   70, 74
.pop()   94
.quantile()   77, 105
.replace()   15, 17
.resample()   77, 102
.resample().first()   77
.resample().last()   78
.resample().mean()   78

.reset_index()   96
.sort_values()   96, 101
.sort()   19
.std()   76
.sum()   100
.summary()   109
.to_csv()   71
.transpose()   91
.upper()   19
.values()   94

A
ACF (autocorrelation function)   120
ADF (augumented Dickey-Fuller)   123
AIC (Akaike Infomration Criterion)   124
alpha, α 53, 110, 113
amortization   61
Anaconda   1
and   22
API   73, 89
AR(1)   119
argument of a function   5
ARIMA   124
ARMA   119, 129
assignment   7
autoregressive   119
autoregressive moving average   119

B
backtesting   81
beta, β 110
BIC (Bayesian Information Criterion)   124

Black-Scholes Model	61
Black, Fischer	61
BND, Bond Market ETF	49, 79
bond pricing	48
bool, Boolean	6, 21, 22
break	28
C	
Caesar Cipher	19, 37
CAPM (Captial Asset Pricing Model)	110
card	41
Cartesian coordinate	51
chr()	19
concatenate	13
Console	29
constraint	137
contrarian	86
correlation coefficient	48, 133
coupon	48
coupon rate	61
D	
DataFrame	65, 74
datetime library	115
del	18
dice	39
Dickey-Fuller test	123
dict, dictionary	18, 89, 93
distribution	39
drift in Dickey-Fuller test	123
dt.datetime()	115
E	
Efficient Frontier	48, 54, 135
elif	22
else	22
exec()	89
exercise price	61
expected return of an asset	133
expression	5
F	
face value of a bond	61
FileNotFound	65
filter rule	82
float()	9
floating number	5
flush	42, 47
for loop	33
forecast error	129
four of a kind	41, 47
FRED	116
French, Ken	110
full house	41, 47
function	5, 45
function return	45
G	
Gates, Bill	42
Google Finance	62, 73
grid line	54
grid search	136
groupby	99
H	
hashtag	9
histogram	53
I	
IDE	1
if statement	21
immutable	15
immutable sequence	14
implied volatility	62
import	25
incremental increase	58
indentation	22
indexing	14
initial value	58

input()	8
int()	9
integer	5
internal rate of return	61
IPython Console	1
iShares Core S&P Mid-Cap ETF	112
iterator	35
K	
kennel	29
keys	93
L	
len()	14, 35
list	16
list literal	134
list()	18
literal	94
logical test	21
logistic regression	107, 113
logit function	113
M	
market risk premium	110
Markowitz, Harry	142
matplotlib.pyplot	51, 70
maximization	133
McKinney, Wes	65
mean	40
method	15
minimization	133
minimize()	139
minimum variance portfolio	140
Missing values	67
modularization	45
modulus operator	7
momentum	86
Monte Carlo simulation	39, 60
moving average	84

moving average crossover	84
MSE (Mean Squared Errors)	130
mutable	16
N	
N/A	68
NLSY	107
natural logrithm	62
New column creation	67
non-stationary	122
None	46
normal distribution	40
not in	24
np.dot()	141
np.exp()	62
np.log()	62
np.matrix()	141
np.mean()	41
np.multiply()	141
np.ones()	141
np.random.choice()	36
number	5
numerical method	57
numpy library	25, 36, 41
O	
object	5
objective function	137
odds	42
OLS regression	107, 142
operator	5
optimization	133
option pricing	61
or	23
ord()	19
out-of-sample forecast	129
P	
pair	41, 48

Pandas	65, 74
pandas_datareader library	96, 116
par	48
parameter of a function	5
pd.concat()	91
pd.DataFrame()	70, 91, 102
pd.merge()	96
pd.read_csv()	65, 74, 99
PEDMA	6
pivot table	99
plot color	52
plot labeling	53
plot marker	52
plot tick	54
plot title	53
plt.bar()	95
plt.figure()	53
plt.hist()	53
plt.plot()	51
plt.title()	95
plt.xticks()	95
pointer	8
poker	42, 47
portfolio management	40
print()	5
probability	39
Q	
quadratic equation	47, 58
R	
R	65
random library	36, 40
random walk	55, 122, 130
random.gauss()	40
random.randint()	36, 40, 42, 60
random.random()	134
range()	33, 34
repl.it	1
risk-free interest rate	61, 110
rolling regression	115
roulette	42
S	
Scholes, Myron	61
scipy	137
scipy.stats library	62
sequence	14
Series	66
simple moving average	84
slicing	14, 68
SLSQP	139
sm.acf()	120
sm.add_constant()	109
sm.adfuller()	123
sm.ARMA()	119
sm.Logit()	114
sm.OLS()	109
sm.OLS().fit()	109
SMA	84
sorting	24, 25
spreadsheet	65
SPY, SPDR S&P 500 ETF	42, 49, 78, 99
spyder	1
sse (sum of squared errors)	142
standard deviation	40, 48
stationarity	120
statsmodels.api	107
statsmodels.tsa.api	119
str()	13
straight	42, 47
straight flush	47
strike price	61
string	13
summary statistics	76

T

technical analysis	81
Tesla	73
text	13
three of a kind	41, 48
time series	54, 77, 119
time trend in Dickey-Fuller test	123
time.sleep()	31
trend following	84
tuple	18
two pair	48
type	5

U

uniform distribution	40
unit root	122

V

values	93
variance of an asset's return	133
varirance-covariance matrix	140
VIX	62

W

web.DataReader()	104
while loop	27
working directory	65

X

x-y scatter plot	51
xkcd	145

Y

Yahoo Finance	62, 73, 89, 116
yield to maturity	48, 61

Z

zip()	94

Made in the USA
Middletown, DE
21 February 2020

85116492R00086